Number 102
Summer 2004

New Directions for Evaluation

Jean A. King
Editor-in-Chief

Robin Miller
Katherine Ryan
Nancy Zajano
Associate Editors

In Search of Cultural Competence in Evaluation

Toward Principles and Practices

Melva Thompson-Robinson
Rodney Hopson
Saumitra SenGupta
Editors

IN SEARCH OF CULTURAL COMPETENCE IN EVALUATION: TOWARD PRINCIPLES
AND PRACTICES
Melva Thompson-Robinson, Rodney Hopson, Saumitra SenGupta (eds.)
New Directions for Evaluation, no. 102
Jean A. King, Editor-in-Chief
Copyright ©2004 Wiley Periodicals, Inc., A Wiley company

Microfilm copies of issues and articles are available in 16mm and 35mm,
as well as microfiche in 105mm, through University Microfilms Inc., 300
North Zeeb Road, Ann Arbor, Michigan 48106-1346.

New Directions for Evaluation is indexed in Contents Pages in Education,
Higher Education Abstracts, and Sociological Abstracts.

NEW DIRECTIONS FOR EVALUATION (ISSN 1097-6736, electronic ISSN 1534-
875X) is part of The Jossey-Bass Education Series and is published quarterly by Wiley Subscription Services, Inc., a Wiley company, at
Jossey-Bass, 989 Market Street, San Francisco, California 94103-1741.

SUBSCRIPTIONS cost $80.00 for U.S./Canada/Mexico; $104 international.
For institutions, agencies, and libraries, $175 U.S.; $215 Canada; $249
international. Prices subject to change.

EDITORIAL CORRESPONDENCE should be addressed to the Editor-in-Chief,
Jean A. King, University of Minnesota, 330 Wulling Hall, 86 Pleasant
Street SE, Minneapolis, MN 55455.

www.josseybass.com

Editorial Policy and Procedures

New Directions for Evaluation, a quarterly sourcebook, is an official publication of the American Evaluation Association. The journal publishes empirical, methodological, and theoretical works on all aspects of evaluation. A reflective approach to evaluation is an essential strand to be woven through every volume. The editors encourage volumes that have one of three foci: (1) craft volumes that present approaches, methods, or techniques that can be applied in evaluation practice, such as the use of templates, case studies, or survey research; (2) professional issue volumes that present issues of import for the field of evaluation, such as utilization of evaluation or locus of evaluation capacity; (3) societal issue volumes that draw out the implications of intellectual, social, or cultural developments for the field of evaluation, such as the women's movement, communitarianism, or multiculturalism. A wide range of substantive domains is appropriate for *New Directions for Evaluation;* however, the domains must be of interest to a large audience within the field of evaluation. We encourage a diversity of perspectives and experiences within each volume, as well as creative bridges between evaluation and other sectors of our collective lives.

The editors do not consider or publish unsolicited single manuscripts. Each issue of the journal is devoted to a single topic, with contributions solicited, organized, reviewed, and edited by a guest editor. Issues may take any of several forms, such as a series of related chapters, a debate, or a long article followed by brief critical commentaries. In all cases, the proposals must follow a specific format, which can be obtained from the editor-in-chief. These proposals are sent to members of the editorial board and to relevant substantive experts for peer review. The process may result in acceptance, a recommendation to revise and resubmit, or rejection. However, the editors are committed to working constructively with potential guest editors to help them develop acceptable proposals.

Jean A. King, Editor-in-Chief
University of Minnesota
330 Wulling Hall
86 Pleasant Street SE
Minneapolis, MN 55455
e-mail: kingx004@umn.edu

CONTENTS

Editors' Notes

With increasing emphasis on matters pertaining to race, culture, and diversity at the professional level and the currency of these topics in our larger social context in the United States, this volume discusses how the evaluation field can integrate notions of cultural competence into evaluation theory, policy, practice, and methodology. Guiding this discussion is the construct of cultural competence, which has been defined in numerous ways across a variety of fields of study (Thompson, 1998). As we evaluators learn about the contributions of colleagues in other fields to an understanding of cultural competence, we come to appreciate the critical applicability of these ideas to our own domain of theory and practice.

At a basic level, cultural competence is appreciation and recognition of other cultural groups and acceptance of the inherent differences that exist among them. At its highest level, cultural competence involves designing appropriate programs, standards, interventions, and measures so that they are specific, relevant, and valid for each unique group. In counseling psychology, for instance, Stanley Sue's search for cultural competence (1990) has clear implications for the search for cultural competence in evaluation. Within Sue's domain, the challenges of delivering mental health services to culturally diverse ethnic minority groups are well recognized; they include developing valid assessments, appropriate treatments, and meaningful rapport. In response to these challenges, nearly a decade ago the American Psychological Association established guidelines that would facilitate more culturally responsive treatments, including "skills, knowledge and practices that are attuned to the unique worldviews and cultural backgrounds of clients by striving to incorporate understanding of a client's ethnic, linguistic, racial and cultural backgrounds into therapy" (APA, 2003, p. 391).

In evaluation, the work of Anna-Marie Madison (1992), Donna Mertens (1999), Karen Kirkhart (1995), Stafford Hood (1998, 1999), and others have argued that cultural competence in evaluation is rooted in how evaluators attend to issues of diversity, cultural responsiveness, and multicultural validity. For instance, we highlight Kirkhart's 1994 presidential address as a watershed moment for discussion of cultural competence in the evaluation field. When she acknowledged that we evaluators "turn our knowledge, attitudes, and skills surrounding multicultural connections inward, reflexively, to our own profession" (1995, p. 8), she implied that we have an important role to play in capturing multiple cultural perspectives in the field in order to promote social justice and equity.

The conceptual work of Edmund Gordon (1977) and others (see the responses by Ernie House, 1999; Michael Patton, 1999; and Rodney Hopson, 1999, to John Stanfield's 1998 American Evaluation Association plenary address) frames new questions about race, power, and minority issues in evaluation and how these issues are paramount to our understanding of cultural competence in evaluation. These new questions and frames lead us to search for alternative epistemological explanations when describing and evaluating experiences of communities and people of color, all the while reexamining the historical role of program evaluation in portraying diverse cultural and ethnic communities. If the evaluation field is to really attend to pertinent and valuable "multicultural connections," as Kirkhart challenges us, in the twenty-first century, then the study and advancement of culturally competent evaluation must be realized as a central issue facing the field.

Within the broad context of cultural competence and evaluation, the editors of this volume offer an important distinction between culturally competent evaluation and the evaluation of cultural competence. Clearly, circumstances exist where both concepts are intertwined, especially in evaluating cultural competence. In the evaluation of cultural competence it is hard to imagine that an evaluation plan would be completely devoid of its own cultural competence considerations and methods. Although the editors agree that issues related to both culturally competent evaluation and the evaluation of cultural competence need to be furthered explored, the editors have chosen to focus this volume on culturally competent evaluation. We strongly encourage others to pursue the discussion of evaluation of culturally competent services.

In examining culturally competent evaluation, this volume is shaped by several questions:

- How does culture matter in evaluation theory *and* practice?
- How does attention to cultural issues make for better evaluation practice?
- What is the "value-addedness" of cultural competence in evaluation?
- How do the complexities, challenges, and politics of diversity issues affect evaluation?

The opening chapter of this volume, by SenGupta, Hopson, and Thompson-Robinson, offers a broad definition of *culture* and *cultural competence* that frames the other discussions in the volume. This introductory chapter synthesizes ideas about cultural competence from other disciplines and professions, extends these ideas to evaluation, and asserts the value-addedness of cultural competence in the evaluation field.

At times, evaluators find themselves evaluating programs that do not explicitly purport to incorporate cultural competence as a major goal or objective but nevertheless call for culturally sensitive and culturally competent evaluation. Several chapters in this volume provide case studies of what cultural competence means to diverse cultural groups in the United States and how evaluations affecting those groups were made culturally competent. Authors also share pitfalls and recommendations for implementing culturally competent evaluation. Hood's chapter examines the meaning and shaping of culturally competent evaluation through the eyes of an African American evaluator. LaFrance's chapter explores what cultural competence means when working in Indian Country, offering conceptual and methodological challenges that can arise when working with this population. Conner's chapter focuses on his work with Latino populations by describing how two programs and evaluations were culturally crafted to target populations. These specific cases imply that a focus on racial or ethnic groups is not monolithic and reveals some complicated matters as they pertain to cultural competence in evaluation-making decisions.

Notwithstanding policy changes at the federal, state, and local levels to address ethnic and cultural issues in health and education, in particular there remains a lack of critical discussion in the literature on some of the policy making, implementation, and evaluation implications that are central to cultural competence. In their chapter, King, Nielsen, and Colby propose competencies that represent cultural competence in evaluation, on the basis of their experience evaluating multicultural initiatives in school districts in the Midwest. Zulli and Frierson then share their experience evaluating a precollege and recruitment program in diverse student communities and describe how the evaluation plan was influenced by culture. In the last chapter, Symonette offers suggestions on how these issues about cultural competence advance a multicultural diversity agenda in higher education, using her case study from the University of Wisconsin Administration System Office of Multicultural Affairs.

The themes of this volume imply that the domains of diversity and difference, multicultural sensitivity, cultural responsiveness, and competence remain complex, multifaceted, and context-rich and are ripe for discussion and application in the evaluation enterprise. The timeliness of the volume offers evaluators in the United States and abroad connection with and thinking about ways to apply cultural sensitivity, responsiveness, and competence in contemporary evaluation practice.

Melva Thompson-Robinson
Rodney Hopson
Saumitra SenGupta
Editors

References

American Psychological Association. "Guidelines on Multicultural Education, Training, Research, Practice, and Organizational Change for Psychologists." *American Psychologist*, 2003, 58(8), 377–402.

Gordon, E. W. "Diverse Human Populations and Problems in Educational Program Evaluation via Achievement Testing." In M. J. Wargo and D. R. Green (eds.), *Achievement Testing of Disadvantaged and Minority Students for Educational Program Evaluation.* New York: McGraw-Hill, 1977.

Hood, S. "Responsive Evaluation Amistad Style: Perspectives of One African-American Evaluator." Paper presented at the Robert E. Stake Symposium on Educational Evaluation, University of Illinois, Champaign, Ill., 1998.

Hood, S. "Culturally Responsive Performance-Based Assessment: Conceptual and Psychometric Considerations." *Journal of Negro Education,* 1999, *67,* 187–196.

Hopson, R. K. "Minority Issues in Evaluation Revisited: Reconceptualizing and Creating Opportunities for Institutional Change." *American Journal of Evaluation,* 1999, *20*(3), 445–451.

House, E. R. "Evaluation and People of Color: A Response to Professor Stanfield." *American Journal of Evaluation,* 1999, *20*(3), 433–435.

Kirkhart, K. E. "Seeking Multicultural Validity: A Postcard from the Road." *Evaluation Practice,* 1995, *16,* 1–12.

Madison, A.-M. (ed.). *Minority Issues in Program Evaluation.* New Directions for Program Evaluation, no. 53. San Francisco: Jossey-Bass, 1992.

Mertens, D. "Inclusive Evaluation: Implications of Transformative Theory for Evaluation." *American Journal of Evaluation,* 1999, *20,* 1–14.

Patton, M. Q. "Some Framing Questions About Racism and Evaluation: Thoughts Stimulated by Professor Stanfield's 'Slipping Through the Front Door.'" *American Journal of Evaluation,* 1999, *20*(3), 437–443.

Stanfield, J. H. "Slipping Through the Front Door: Relevant Social Scientific Evaluation in the People of Color Century." *American Journal of Evaluation,* 1999, *20*(3), 415–431.

Sue, S. "In Search of Cultural Competence in Psychotherapy and Counseling." *American Psychologist,* 1990, *53*(4), 440–448.

Thompson, M. "Culturally Competent Service in Public Health Settings: Development of a Conceptual Framework and Assessment Methodology." Unpublished Dr.P.H. dissertation, 1998.

MELVA THOMPSON-ROBINSON is an assistant professor of behavioral science and health education in the Institute of Public Health in the College of Pharmacy and Pharmaceutical Sciences at Florida A&M University in Tallahassee.

RODNEY HOPSON is an associate professor and interim chair of the Department of Foundations and Leadership in the School of Education and a faculty member in the Center for Interpretive and Qualitative Research at Duquesne University in Pittsburgh.

SAUMITRA SENGUPTA is a research scientist at the Behavioral Health Research Center of the Southwest in Albuquerque, New Mexico.

1

This chapter is an overview of the understanding of cultural competence and context in evaluation, highlighting how other disciplines have addressed the importance of culture and suggesting the value-addedness of culture to program evaluation and design.

Cultural Competence in Evaluation: An Overview

Saumitra SenGupta, Rodney Hopson, Melva Thompson-Robinson

> My mission was clearly scripted: to treat the seriously mentally ill—those unfortunate individuals with schizophrenia, manic-depressive illness, depression, and serious anxiety disorders. After expending plenty of time, money, and effort learning conventional American medicine, I needed to deprogram myself from its reliance on deductive reasoning to solve medical problems while in Zimbabwe. I needed to unlock my intuitive mind, opening it to the mysterious realms of subculture and spirituality in order to work as a psychiatrist in this new culture. I didn't have to junk those four years of medical school and another four years of psychiatric residency. I prescribed medications, performed physical examination, and made accurate diagnoses as per the fourth edition of the American Psychiatric Association's *Diagnostic and Statistical Manual of Mental Disorders (DSM-IV)*. But to go to Zimbabwe and simply apply *DSM-IV* and the American medical worldview would have been naïve and inaccurate.
> —Paul R. Linde (2001, pp. 53–54)

Evaluation inarguably takes place within social, cultural, historical, economic, and political contexts—the contexts defined by human existence and experience (APA, 2003). These contexts envelope many dimensions. Race, ethnicity, language, gender, age, religion, and sexual orientation are

---

The authors greatly appreciate Jennifer Greene's careful review and constructive feedback in writing this chapter.

among the commonly listed demographic attributes of contextual diversity. Not so commonly discussed in conversations about evaluation are the contextual dimensions of power, economy, living situation, and class, among other denominators of equity and sociopolitical status, *and* the contextual dimensions specific to culture.

That is, despite the recent flurry of activity and discussion in a number of disciplines meant to lift issues of culture and cultural context to the fore of discovery, theory, and application, the evaluation field has lagged behind. Yet culture is an undeniably integral part of the diverse contexts of evaluation, and therefore an integral part of evaluation. Culture is present in evaluation not only in the contexts in which programs are implemented but also in the designs of these programs and the approach, stance, or methods evaluators choose to use in their work. A common thread between culture and evaluation is the concept of *values*. Culture shapes values, beliefs, and worldviews. Evaluation is fundamentally an endeavor of determining values, merit, and worth. In making the case for cultural competence in evaluation, this chapter emphasizes this common thread.

The concept of culture itself is popularly considered in terms of such manifest activities as food, music, celebrations, holidays, dance, and dress and clothing. However, such manifestations are rooted in inherent beliefs and value orientations that influence customs, norms, practices, and social institutions, including psychological processes, language, caretaking practices, media, educational systems, and organizations (Fiske, Kitayama, Markus, and Nisbett, 1998). The APA's multicultural guidelines (2003) posit that culture is the embodiment of a worldview through learned and transmitted beliefs, values, and practices, including religious and spiritual traditions. It also encompasses a way of living informed by the historical, economic, ecological, and political forces acting on a group.

Understanding these underlying dimensions of culture leads to recognizing value differences, and sometimes value conflicts, that go beyond simple demographic differences and move into such dimensions as intergenerational, socioeconomic, and other group identity characteristics. Lee (1997) offers an example of how cultural differences lead to value contrasts. She identifies the contrast between a set of parallel values drawn from Eastern (predominantly agricultural) and Western (predominantly industrial) values (Table 1.1). It is readily apparent that such values permeate policies, programs, and evaluations alike. For instance, in environmental policy analysis, whether the analyst holds a perspective of mastery of nature or living in harmony with nature significantly influences the character and content of his or her analysis.

Evaluation practice is largely driven by policy decisions, including funding, and by programmatic needs such as service delivery. The literature in these areas has already moved to embracing a deeper view of culture that includes discussion of the inherent power structure in society and the role the dominant culture plays in shaping the debate. Policy decisions and service

Table 1.1. Contrasting Values Underlying Cultural Differences in East and West

Eastern Agricultural System: Values of Traditional Society Values	Western Industrialized System: Values of Modern Society
Family and group oriented	Individual orientation
Extended family	Nuclear or blended family
Multiple parenting	Couple parenting
Primary relationship: parent-child bond	Primary relationship: marital bond
Emphasis on interpersonal relationships	Emphasis on self-fulfillment and self-development
Status and relationships determined by age and role in family	Status achieved by individual's efforts
Well-defined family member roles	Flexible family member roles
Favoritism toward males	Increasing opportunities for females
Authoritarian orientation	Democratic orientation
Suppression of emotions	Expression of emotions
Fatalism, karma	Personal control over the environment
Harmony with nature	Mastery over nature
Cooperative orientation	Competition orientation
Spiritualism	Materialism and consumerism
Past, present, and future orientation	Present and future orientation

Source: Adapted from Lee (1997, p. 9).

delivery systems are also the primary venues where the cultural contexts are operationalized first. Therefore attention to the cultural contexts of policy and program development is needed before discussing the cultural contexts of evaluation. Accordingly, this overview is divided into two main sections: a discussion of the cultural contexts of policy, program, and service delivery; and a look at the implications for evaluation, where the debate currently stands in terms of both evaluation theory and methodology, and an attempt to define what culturally competent evaluation means when one takes these viewpoints into account. The chapter concludes with examples of what is happening in evaluation practice in terms of incorporating cultural competence, and what still needs to be done.

Cultural Contexts of Policymaking, Program Development, and Service Delivery

In several important areas, culture defines the context and language in which the policies are framed, program theory developed, and programs implemented. Often the policy discourse and formulation stem from identification of a lack or a problem. This section discusses the role of culture from problem definition to program implementation and how cultural competence has been defined in the programmatic context.

Culture in Problem Definition and Program Theory. Developments in the areas of program and service delivery systems design in the last decade have begun to underscore the importance of recognizing, understanding, and appreciating the cultural contexts in which programs operate. This is evident in the evolving conceptualizations of health, mental health, education, and social service program models. For instance, in K–12 education, cultural heritage and immigration generational status have been identified as factors to consider when developing educational media and curricula (Suzuki and Valencia, 1997). Similarly, in counseling and therapy there has been extensive discussion of how individuals' worldviews and life experiences often manifest themselves in presenting symptoms, the meaning of illness in life, motivation and willingness to seek treatment, and perseverance in treatment (see APA, 2003).

More broadly, because values are so integral to culture they are also integral to cultural dimensions of program design. One key site for the cultural expression of values is in how social problems and the programs intended to address them are conceptualized. It is also in this context that one needs to be especially aware of the dangers of imposition, misinterpretation, and misrepresentation of values, of viewing a particular context with a different cultural lens in program design. Values and worldviews that are informed by one's own culture are formidable. Patton (1985) notes that the power of culture makes us relatively oblivious to the limitation of our own perspectives, behaviors, and values. Parham (2002) and Madison (1992) discuss the pitfalls of normative models, whereby the models construed from "other" cultural and belief systems are often viewed as deficient. Madison, for instance, cautions against dominant cultural interpretations and unidimensional cultural orientations of the world explaining those of multicultural participants and stakeholders. She suggests that "the cultural biases inherent in how middle-class white researchers interpret the experiences of low-income minorities may lead to erroneous assumptions and faulty propositions concerning causal relationships, to invalid social theory, and consequently to invalid program theory" (1992, p. 38). This is a clear warning that evaluators themselves should be wary of culture-free evaluative inferences.

In discussing the conceptualization of social problems, Madison (1992) emphasizes that the most important role program participants can play is in program design and planning, and preferably also in problem definition. She convincingly argues that problem definition, a core activity that drives ameliorative program development, is often a dominant culture's interpretation of reality that perpetuates the myth of the deficit model. This has also been echoed by various authors in counseling (Parham and Parham, 2002), social theories (Hage, 1972; Kaplan, 1964), and evaluation literature (House, 1983, 1999). Examples include program theories framed by such terms as *underprivileged, at-risk, chronically unemployed,* and *chronically homeless.* Madison (2000) describes an at-risk youth program where some probing from the program planners and administrators revealed that most of the needs identification and program planning were based on stereotypical and negative views about the families and cultural attributes of the population to be served. In an article describing an HIV/AIDS prevention program, Hopson, Lucas, and Peterson (2000) further show serious discordance in understanding of the issues among the stakeholders that, when clarified, led to a better program design.

Culture in Policy Discourse and Decisions. House (1999) presents an analysis of policymaking in the United States and the seeming contradiction between deep-seated beliefs about democracy, equality, and fairness on the one hand and lack of comprehension by "white" Americans of the extent to which racism exists in this country on the other. From sociologist Wilson's contention (1987) that Americans are unlikely to support policies believed to primarily benefit minorities but support the ones perceived to benefit all Americans, House comes up with a corollary that Americans support policies harmful to minorities that they would not tolerate if those policies were applied to majority populations. He cites educational retention policies as an example of this corollary since minority students are much more likely to be retained in grade than majority students. House provides a scathing assessment of the education system in this country in that inherently racist and biased policies go unnoticed behind the appearance of equality. He characterizes the system as one of institutional racism, whereby racism can persist even in the absence of hostile racist thoughts.

Policies influence and often control funding streams that support program development and service delivery. The funding streams may be based on a needs assessment model, where needs are construed as problems or deficits. This runs counter to a strengths-based approach in which the community's strengths and assets are identified and reinforced in program design. The entire program planner and administrator class in human services has been inculcated in the methodologies of needs assessment, a strategy Patton (2000) points out as having become all too powerful to recognize the strengths or assets in the community or among the program participants. On the one hand, one can see why funding should be driven by particular needs, but on the other hand a programming ideology dominated by such reasoning makes it difficult to obtain funding for initiatives that actually work to identify individual and community strengths, and then further them in a visionary way toward social betterment. In health care, this kind of funding bias is exemplified by the dearth of funding for prevention and primary care programs. The health care safety net in the United States is disproportionately directed toward emergency and life support services, rather than providing timely primary care and preventive services to those who need them. The disease-based medical system that drives such funding formulas is another example of the "fixing the deficit" approach that fails to recognize the value of cultural and contextual strengthening approaches.

Cultural Competence in Policy and Program Development. Cultural competence has been defined in the social program literature from a systemic viewpoint. Although the cultural attributes of mental illness have been recognized for a long time, the roles of culture and cross-cultural situations in assessment, diagnosis, and therapy were extensively recognized by the American Psychiatric Association in the *Diagnostic and Statistical Manual of Mental Disorders* (APA, 1994) and in a supplement to the U.S. Surgeon General's report (U.S.DHHS, 2001). In 1989, Cross, Bazron, Dennis, and Isaacs offered a definition of cultural competence in the children's mental health system that is widely quoted in the human service literature: "A set of congruent behaviors, attitudes and policies that come together as a system, agency or among professionals and enable that system, agency or those professionals to work effectively in cross-cultural situations" (p. iv).

The operational details of such a definition are being worked out in policy formulation, building practice skills, and evolving behaviors and attitudes of the practitioner in the service delivery system. In psychology, detailed guidelines have been published that deal with both practice and research (see APA, 2003; CNPAAEMI, 2000; APA 1990). One emerging theme in this development has been an elevation of the importance of practitioners' recognizing culture-specific strengths and uniqueness. Taking counseling and therapy as an example, the progress in cultural competence in practice is evidenced by further literature addressing specific ethnicities such as African Americans (Parham, 2002) and Asian Americans (Lee, 1997).

Cultural Context in Evaluation

This section builds on the discussion of cultural competence in the policy and program arena and constructs a definition of cultural competence in evaluation, including methodological and ethical considerations.

The Common Thread of Values. An examination of the cultural context of evaluation is best initiated by looking at the common thread between culture and evaluation. The concept of *values* is a fundamental aspect of evaluation. Classical evaluation theorists such as Scriven (1991) define evaluation as determining the merit, worth, or value of things. In his view, this is what separates evaluation from social science research, which, he argues, "does not establish standards or values" (Coffman, 2004, p. 7). Similarly, Stufflebeam (2003) describes values as the core of an evaluative endeavor.

According to House and Howe (2000, p. 8), "Evaluation is a procedure for determining values, which are emergent and transformed through deliberative processes into evaluation findings." Critical analysis of the use of value systems, including perceived biases and problems associated with them, has also emerged in the social science research literature. For instance, Pettigrew (1979) argues that unexamined in-group and out-group values contrast can lead to attributional error whereby the in-group characteristics are often viewed in an overly positive light and the out-group ones in a more negative fashion. The evaluator also needs to be cognizant of not losing track of the values systems because too much focus is placed on the means to derive the value judgment. Greene (2000) uses the phrase *masking of values by methods* to describe the situation where the stakeholder's valuing of different outcomes is overcome by methodological discussions that essentially dislocate the evaluative endeavor from its fundamental mission.

Cultural Competence in Evaluation: Continuing the Conversation. The field of evaluation has a long road to go in incorporating cultural context in its everyday practice. Various aspects of broader cultural issues have begun to be addressed, but the term *cultural competence* has not been commonly used to characterize evaluator competence in incorporating cultural context in evaluation. An examination of the titles of evaluation publications in the last two decades demonstrates this. Culture and evaluation (Patton, 1985), cross-cultural evaluation (Ginsberg, 1988; Merryfield, 1985), responsive evaluation (Hood, 2001; Stake, 1975), social justice issues (House, 1993), minority issues in evaluation (Hopson, 1999; Madison, 1992), social justice and multicultural validity (Kirkhart, 1995), inclusive evaluation (Mertens, 1999), race and institutional racism (House, 1999), deliberative democratic evaluation (House and Howe, 2000), culturally responsive evaluation (Frierson, Hood, and Hughes, 2002), and multicultural evaluation (Hopson, 2004; Kagawa-Singer and others, 2003) all deal with cultural contexts of evaluation and in some cases offer the tools to implement culturally related theoretical perspectives in evaluation.

It is worth noting that some of the recent papers in this list have critically analyzed earlier works and started to frame the issue in a culturally responsive framework. For instance, Hopson (1999) asked what the term *minority issues* really means and whether the term itself has the unintended consequence of marginalizing cultural values and strengths. Hopson lays out an analysis of the themes that emerge once minority issues are examined from a cultural lens and proposes the need for creating a new and positive framework for evaluation theory and practice that recognizes and incorporates the cultural context. Hood (2001) and Frierson, Hood, and Hughes (2002) present such a new framework underscoring responsiveness and building upon the earlier works of Stake (1975) by explicitly discussing the cultural context.

One hallmark of evaluative responsiveness as framed by these authors is the evaluator's active recognition, appreciation, and incorporation of culturally related contextual factors into his or her practice. The contextual factors include many of the more readily discussed dimensions of culture, including the demographics and some aspects of socioeconomic factors. But these factors also include the less spoken issues of power, institutional racism, and social justice.

Theorists such as House (1999) address these issues directly in terms of both policy and implications for evaluation (House and Howe, 2000). In discussing the implications for evaluation of incorporating contextual factors related to institutional power and equity issues, House and Howe point out the need to address them through deliberation, inclusion, and dialogue.

They make two important points. First, in an ideal world, democratic institutions imply the existence of deliberation and dialogue, but this is not the case in the real world. The evaluator needs to proactively engage these democratic practices in a cognizant manner. Second, House and Howe emphasize the importance of implementation. Though noting the idealistic nature of the terms *deliberation* and *dialogue,* they advocate the proactive use of these terms in guiding the planning and implementation of an evaluative endeavor.

Joh, Endo, and Yu (2003) note that there is some hesitation among evaluation scholars and practitioners to define what cultural competence in evaluation means. However, examination of ideas related to cultural responsiveness and consideration of contextual factors bring some initial clarity to understanding and defining the concept. Cultural competence in evaluation rests on active awareness, understanding, and appreciation for the context at hand, and it uses responsive and inclusive means to conduct evaluation. The main driving force behind cultural competence is the growing recognition that in a pluralistic society situations involving evaluators and evaluees from different cultures, as well as cultural diversity among the evaluees, are inevitable. In such situations, the best hope for conducting an evaluation lies in increased cultural competence on the part of the evaluators.

Merryfield (1985) began to address the issue of cultural competence in the context of cross-cultural evaluation, in particular in the international evaluation arena. She identified some basic problems and proposed some solutions to these issues. Among the problems she identified were cultural differences, inapplicability of Western methods in a non-Western setting, and various ethical issues. Among the possible solutions, she listed use of a variety of strategies and sources, involving host country people, and using a team approach that includes culture specialists.

The problems and possible solutions identified by Merryfield are not without implications for domestic evaluation. In comparing an international evaluation project and a domestic one, Conner (1985) argues that "international evaluation provides insights about some of the important but typically unconscious assumptions that underlie—and sometimes undermine—the conduct of our everyday evaluation work" (p. 19). For instance, Merryfield's prescriptions for involving host country people and for using a team approach can quite easily be translated in the domestic context. These are exemplified by Laurine Thomas's evaluation capacity building work in the Mississippi Delta (Thomas, Rogers, and Fraser, 2000); Ross Conner's HIV/AIDS prevention program evaluation work in the Latino communities (in this volume); and Hopson, Lucas, and Peterson's work on understanding discourse in HIV/AIDS prevention work in the African American communities (2000).

Merryfield's call for a variety of strategies and resources as part of culturally competent evaluation practice is echoed by Wadsworth (2001). She calls for a range of methods, including not-so-common methods that are "needed to bring out the tacit, to surface the undiscussables, the repressed and suppressed, or to illuminate deeper values or structures operating" (p. 47). Wadsworth (2001) ventures further to define evaluation as dialogue across difference and distance. In this context Wadsworth distinguishes between evaluation that *seeks* (open or inquiry) and evaluation that *checks* (audit review). This quality of openness is important to ideas of culturally competent evaluation. More generally, the open, dialogical, deliberative, and democratic approaches to evaluation (Ryan and DeStefano, 2000; Wadsworth, 2001) and the challenges thereof—including the possibilities of key stakeholder absence and limited evaluator authority (Greene, 2000)—are all germane to the concept of cultural competence in evaluation in that addressing issues of power in evaluation constitutes a significant task.

In addition to actively engaging the existing power structure and employing a variety of strategies, methods, and resources, it is critical for the culturally competent evaluator to practice constant self-examination of values, assumptions, and cultural contexts. What Wadsworth (2001) calls "immersed engagement" has been discussed in therapeutic practice by Parham (2002). Indeed, there are concepts discussed in the counseling literature that have relevance in advancing culturally competent evaluation practice. Parham identifies four stages of evolution using the concept of social distance in cross-racial therapy situations: pre-encounter, encounter, immersion-emersion, and internalization. He argues that the best therapeutic alliance is achieved when the therapist-client duo are in an internalization stage of social distance where each is comfortable with his or her own cultural identity and the other's, and ready for the true therapy to begin. This is reflected in the first APA guideline (APA, 2003) on commitment to cultural awareness and knowledge of self and others: "Psychologists are encouraged to recognize that, as cultural beings, they may hold attitudes and beliefs that can detrimentally influence their perceptions of and interactions with individuals who are ethnically and racially different from others" (p. 382).

From this varied conversation about culture, context, and competence in evaluation (and other fields), the beginnings of a definition of cultural competence in evaluation emerge. Cultural competence in evaluation can be broadly defined as a systematic, responsive inquiry that is actively cognizant, understanding, and appreciative of the cultural context in which the evaluation takes place; that frames and articulates the epistemology of the evaluative endeavor; that employs culturally and contextually appropriate methodology; and that uses stakeholder-generated, interpretive means to arrive at the results and further use of the findings.

This definition incorporates several factors that have been discussed in this chapter. It incorporates the notion of responsiveness to contextual factors with explicit reference to the cultural context. The importance of an appropriate framework and methodology is emphasized in this definition.

Finally, the definition takes into account the means through which evaluation findings are arrived at and used by a culturally competent evaluator. Also implied in this definition but not explicitly mentioned is the concept of ethics in evaluation.

Ethics questions raised by Merryfield in 1985 in cross-cultural evaluation settings are being addressed by the field of evaluation, although much work remains to be done in terms of universal application of proposals put forward by a number of practitioner-theorists. Bamberger (1999) identifies five ethical principles and frames them in the context of multicultural evaluation. He focuses on two particularly thorny issues: (1) the practical aspect of the extent to which the evaluator should respect local customs and values, and (2) how the evaluator can involve stakeholders in international settings. In addressing both these concerns, Bamberger notes some challenges facing participatory empowerment evaluation, the current approach of favor within the enlightened circle of evaluators in cross-cultural settings. For example, how participatory evaluators challenge or ignore the power structure in a given evaluation context can contradict professional principles of respecting other cultures and protecting the legitimate concerns of clients and stakeholders, including such basic items as personal safety. Bamberger offers some useful suggestions for improving the methodological practices in international evaluation, but the thought-provoking article makes it immensely clear there are no black-and-white solutions to the challenges of becoming a culturally competent evaluator. Rather, cultural competence in evaluation is a nuanced endeavor that demands context-specific flexibility and a capacity for understanding and appreciation.

Conclusion

As the quote from Paul Linde at the beginning of this chapter succinctly states, accomplishing cultural competence in one's practice does not mean abandoning one's cultural background, worldview, training, and skill sets. Accomplishing cultural competence requires increased and critical self-reflection as the first building block. In the field of evaluation, one needs to also recognize the pluralistic nature of our endeavor, expand and polish one's tools accordingly, and most important be able to challenge the status quo of the existing power structure as and when needed in order to build a culturally competent practice. However, the individual evaluator cannot be left alone in this venture. The American Evaluation Association (AEA) and the field of evaluation as a whole have significant roles to play. This volume is one building block toward it, and we need to recognize that much remains to be done.

The persistent disconnect between "acceptable" methodologies and the cultural aspects of evaluation remains strong. This is evidenced by various governmental funding opportunities for demonstrating program effectiveness. An example is the recently declared U.S. Department of Education evaluation standards for the No Child Left Behind initiative (U.S. Department of Education, 2003), in which it is stated that "proposed evaluation strategies that use neither experimental designs with random assignment nor quasi-experimental designs using a matched comparison group nor regression discontinuity designs will not be considered responsive to the priority when sufficient numbers of participants are available to support these designs." A similar scenario arises in large-scale federal multisite study designs where a common instrument becomes the primary measurement tool for the overall evaluation design. This is simply incompatible with culturally competent evaluation strategies as discussed in this volume. In the first case, the tenet of employing multiple strategies is grossly violated by the prescriptive, normative methodology selection. In multisite study situations, a vitally important aspect of culturally competent evaluation—that of responsiveness to the context—becomes difficult to accomplish.

One critical need for the profession lies in formulating policies regarding cultural competence in evaluation and developing culturally competent practice guidelines. Cultural competence, by its very nature, calls for a flexible approach to evaluation. However, such an approach still has to be principled, and these principles must be articulated at the professional level. The American Psychological Association (2003) has taken a giant step in officially publishing multicultural guidelines in education, research, and practice of psychology. The section on research guidelines amounts to an excellent starting point for the AEA to consider developing its own guidelines reflecting what culturally competent evaluation would mean in the context of all its topical interest groups. Examples in evaluation can be found in the guidelines for the National Center for Cultural Competence at Georgetown University (Goode and Jones, 2003), which take into account community-related actions. Such a conceptual definition and identification of relevant dimensions remains a major task for the field of evaluation.

A second critical need is development of a critical pool of multicultural, multifaceted evaluators. The former AEA Building Diversity Initiative (AEA, 2000) and internship program with Duquesne University to build the pipeline of evaluators of color are steps in the right direction. However, this is an area where we are all individually, collectively, and professionally responsible for making our practice culturally competent. We must ensure that at our workplaces we are cognizant of this need and that it is reflected in our internship, hiring, and contracting opportunities. One example of this is the effort by Georgetown University's National Center for Cultural Competence to build a consultant pool (Goode and Jones, 2003).

There is an obvious need for more available reports and literature on examples of culturally competent evaluation theory and practice. Again, both the association and the practitioners should take part in this together. In highlighting exemplary practices, literature reviews, and ethical dilemmas, one should set how the issues of cultural competence are addressed as an explicit criterion rather than an unspoken expectation. The California

Endowment's efforts (Joh, Endo, and Yu, 2003; Kagawa-Singer and others, 2003) in developing a knowledge base in culturally competent health evaluation practices is a good example of what can be done in various content areas to develop a literature in culturally competent evaluation. In the academic environment, Arredondo and Hood's work with the annual RACE Conference (2004) is a good model for promoting theory and practice that explicitly deals with cultural issues.

Cultural competence in evaluation is a growing demand in the field. There is a grassroots change happening, fueled by the changing demographics in the United States and global exchanges of unprecedented scale. A lot remains to be done, but the signs of changing times cannot be ignored. The evaluation profession must be a catalyst for change in this new world through acknowledgment, development, and encouragement of culturally competent practice on the part of its members.

References

American Evaluation Association. "Proposal for the Initiative for Building Diversity Among the Evaluation Community, Phase 1." Magnolia, Ark.: American Evaluation Association, 2000.

American Psychiatric Association. *Diagnostic and Statistical Manual of Mental Disorders.* (4th ed.) Washington, D.C.: American Psychiatric Association, 1994.

American Psychological Association. *Guidelines for Providers of Psychological Services to Ethnic, Linguistic, and Culturally Diverse Populations.* Washington, D.C.: American Psychological Association, 1990.

American Psychological Association. "Guidelines on Multicultural Education, Training, Research, Practice, and Organizational Change for Psychologists." *American Psychologist,* 2003, 58(5), 377–402.

Arredondo, P., and Hood, S. "RACE 2004—Relevance of Assessment and Culture in Evaluation," 2004. [http://coe.asu.edu/race/about.html].

Bamberger, M. "Ethical Issues in Conducting Evaluation in International Settings." In J. L. Fitzpatrick and M. Morris (eds.), *Current and Emerging Ethical Challenges in Evaluation.* New Directions for Evaluation, no. 82. San Francisco: Jossey-Bass, 1999.

Coffman, J. "Michael Scriven on the Differences Between Evaluation and Social Science Research." *Harvard Family Research Project—Evaluation Exchange,* 2004, 9(4), 7.

Conner, R. F. "International and Domestic Evaluation: Comparisons and Insights." In M. Q. Patton (ed.), *Culture and Evaluation.* New Directions for Program Evaluation, no. 25. San Francisco: Jossey-Bass, 1985.

Council of National Psychological Associations for the Advancement of Ethnic Minority Interests (CNPAAEMI). *Guidelines for Research in Ethnic Minority Communities.* Washington, D.C.: American Psychological Association, 2000.

Cross, T. L., Bazron, B. J., Dennis, K. W., and Isaacs, M. R. *Towards a Culturally Competent System of Care.* Washington, D.C.: CAASP Technical Assistance Center, Georgetown University Childcare Center, 1989.

Fiske, A. P., Kitayama, S., Markus, H. R., and Nisbett, R. E. "The Cultural Matrix of Social Psychology." In D. T. Gilbert and S. T. Fiske (eds.), *The Handbook of Social Psychology.* (4th ed.) New York: McGraw-Hill, 1998.

Frierson, H., Hood, S., and Hughes, G. "Strategies That Address Culturally Responsive Evaluation." In J. Frechtling (ed.), *The 2002 User-Friendly Handbook for Project Evaluation.* Arlington, Va.: National Science Foundation, 2002.

Ginsberg, P. E. "Evaluation in Cross-Cultural Perspective." *Evaluation and Program Planning,* 1988, *1*(2), 189–195.

Goode, T. D., and Jones, W. "Conceptual Frameworks/Models, Guiding Values and Principles." National Center for Cultural Competence, 2003. [http://gucchd.georgetown.edu/nccc/framework.html].

Greene, J. C. "Challenges in Practicing Deliberative Democratic Evaluation." In K. E. Ryan and L. DeStefano (eds.), *Evaluation as a Democratic Process: Promoting Inclusion, Dialogue, and Deliberation.* New Directions for Evaluation, no. 85. San Francisco: Jossey-Bass, 2000.

Hage, J. *Techniques and Problems of Theory Construction in Sociology.* New York: Wiley, 1972.

Hood, S. "Nobody Knows My Name: In Praise of African American Evaluators Who Were Responsive." In J. C. Greene and T. A. Abma (eds.), *Responsive Evaluation.* New Directions for Evaluation, no. 92. San Francisco: Jossey-Bass, 2001.

Hopson, R. K. "Minority Issues in Evaluation Revisited: Re-conceptualizing and Creating Institutional Change." *American Journal of Evaluation,* 1999, *20*(3), 445–451.

Hopson, R. K. *Overview of Multicultural and Culturally Competent Program Evaluation: Issues, Challenges and Opportunities.* Woodland Hills, Calif.: California Endowment, 2004.

Hopson, R. K., Lucas, K. J., and Peterson, J. A. "HIV/AIDS Talk: Implications for Prevention Intervention and Evaluation." In R. K. Hopson (ed.), *How and Why Language Matters in Evaluation.* New Directions for Evaluation, no. 86. San Francisco: Jossey-Bass, 2000.

House, E. R. "How We Think About Evaluation." In E. R. House (ed.), *Philosophy of Evaluation.* New Directions for Program Evaluation, no. 19. San Francisco: Jossey-Bass, 1983.

House, E. R. *Professional Evaluation: Social Impact and Consequences.* Thousand Oaks, Calif.: Sage, 1993.

House, E. R. "Race and Policy." *Educational Policy Analysis Archives,* 1999, *7*(16). [http://epaa.asu.edu/epaa/v7n16.html].

House, E. R., and Howe, K. R. "Deliberative Democratic Evaluation." In K. E. Ryan and L. DeStefano (eds.), *Evaluation as a Democratic Process: Promoting Inclusion, Dialogue, and Deliberation.* New Directions for Evaluation, no. 85. San Francisco: Jossey-Bass, 2000.

Joh, T., Endo, T., and Yu, H. C. *Voices from the Field: Health and Evaluation Leaders on Multicultural Evaluation.* Woodland Hills, Calif.: California Endowment Foundation, 2003.

Kagawa-Singer, M., and others. *Multicultural Health Evaluation: Literature Review and Critique.* Los Angeles: UCLA School of Public Health, 2003.

Kaplan, A. *The Conduct of Inquiry: Methodology for Behavioral Science.* Scranton, Penn.: Chandler, 1964.

Kirkhart, K. E. "Seeking Multicultural Validity: A Postcard from the Road." *Evaluation Practice,* 1995, *16*(1), 1–12.

Lee, E. "Overview: The Assessment and Treatment of Asian American Families." In E. Lee (ed.), *Working with Asian Americans: A Guide for Clinicians.* New York: Guilford Press, 1997.

Linde, P. R. *Of Spirits and Madness—An American Psychiatrist in Africa.* New York: McGraw-Hill, 2001.

Madison, A. M. "Primary Inclusion of Culturally Diverse Minority Program Participants in the Evaluation Process." In A. M. Madison (ed.), *Minority Issues in Evaluation.* New Directions for Program Evaluation, no. 53. San Francisco: Jossey-Bass, 1992.

Madison, A. M. "Language in Defining Social Problems and in Evaluating Social Programs." In R. K. Hopson (ed.), *How and Why Language Matters in Evaluation.* New Directions for Evaluation, no. 86. San Francisco: Jossey-Bass, 2000.

Merryfield, M. M. "The Challenge of Cross-Cultural Evaluation: Some Views from the Field." In M. Q. Patton (ed.), *Culture and Evaluation*. New Directions for Program Evaluation, no. 25. San Francisco: Jossey-Bass, 1985.

Mertens, D. M. "Inclusive Evaluation: Implications of Transformative Theory for Evaluation." *American Journal of Evaluation*, 1999, *20*(1), 1–14.

Parham, T. A. "Counseling African Americans: The Current State of Affairs." In T. A. Parham (ed.), *Counseling Persons of African Descent: Raising the Bar of Practitioner Competence*. Thousand Oaks, Calif.: Sage, 2002.

Parham, T. A., and Parham W. D. "Understanding African American Mental Health: The Necessity of New Conceptual Paradigms." In T. A. Parham (ed.), *Counseling Persons of African Descent: Raising the Bar of Practitioner Competence*. Thousand Oaks, Calif.: Sage, 2002.

Patton, M. Q. "Cross-Cultural Nongeneralizations." In M. Q. Patton (ed.), *Culture and Evaluation*. New Directions for Program Evaluation, no. 25. San Francisco: Jossey-Bass, 1985.

Patton, M. Q. "Overview: Language Matters." In R. K. Hopson (ed.), *How and Why Language Matters in Evaluation*. New Directions for Evaluation, no. 86. San Francisco: Jossey-Bass, 2000.

Pettigrew, T. G. "The Ultimate Attributional Error: Extending Allport's Cognitive Analysis of Prejudice." *Personality and Social Psychology Bulletin*, 1979, *5*, 461–476.

Ryan, K. E., and DeStefano, L. "Disentangling Dialog: Issues from Practice." In K. E. Ryan and L. DeStefano (eds.), *Evaluation as a Democratic Process: Promoting Inclusion, Dialogue, and Deliberation*. New Directions for Evaluation, no. 85. San Francisco: Jossey-Bass, 2000.

Scriven, M. *Evaluation Thesaurus*. (4th ed.) Thousand Oaks, Calif.: Sage, 1991.

Stake, R. E. "Program Evaluation, Particularly Responsive Evaluation." Kalamazoo, Mich.: Evaluation Center, Western Michigan University, 1975.

Stufflebeam, D. L. "The CIPP Model for Evaluation." In T. Kellaghan and D. L. Stufflebeam (eds.), *The International Handbook of Educational Evaluation*. Norwell, Mass.: Kluwer, 2003.

Suzuki, L. A., and Valencia, R. R. "Race-Ethnicity and Measured Intelligence: Educational Implications." *American Psychologist*, 1997, *52*(10), 1103–1114.

Thomas, L., Rogers, S. J., and Fraser, E. "Building Evaluation Capacity in the Mid-South Delta." Paper presented at the American Evaluation Association Annual Conference, Honolulu, Nov. 2000.

U.S. Department of Education. "Scientifically Based Evaluation Methods." *Federal Register*, RIN 1890-ZA00, 2003.

U.S. Department of Health and Human Services (DHHS). *Mental Health: Culture, Race, and Ethnicity—A Supplement to Mental Health: A Report of the Surgeon General*. Rockville, Md.: Substance Abuse and Mental Health Services Administration, Center for Mental Health Services, U.S. Department of Health and Human Services, 2001.

Wadsworth, Y. "Becoming Responsive—and Some Consequences for Evaluation as Dialogue Across Distance." In J. C. Greene and T. A. Abma (eds.), *Responsive Evaluation*. New Directions for Evaluation, no. 92. San Francisco: Jossey-Bass, 2001.

Wilson, W. J. *The Truly Disadvantaged*. Chicago: University of Chicago Press, 1987.

SAUMITRA SENGUPTA *is a research scientist at the Behavioral Health Research Center of the Southwest in Albuquerque, New Mexico.*

RODNEY HOPSON *is an associate professor and interim chair of the Department of Foundations and Leadership in the School of Education and a faculty member in the Center for Interpretive and Qualitative Research at Duquesne University in Pittsburgh.*

MELVA THOMPSON-ROBINSON *is an assistant professor of behavioral science and health education in the Institute of Public Health in the College of Pharmacy and Pharmaceutical Sciences at Florida A&M University in Tallahassee.*

2

*Taking a historical view of selected program evaluation
approaches, this chapter articulates a personal lens and
journey of understanding how culturally responsive
evaluation is geared toward effectiveness, benefits, and
outcomes of programs designed to serve the less powerful.*

A Journey to Understand the Role of Culture in Program Evaluation: Snapshots and Personal Reflections of One African American Evaluator

Stafford Hood

As is typically the case when I set fingers to keyboard and write about evaluation, my intent is to offer my work and perspective as *one* African American evaluator. The impetus for the thoughts and ideas I express in this chapter were prompted by my preparation to attend and present a paper at the inaugural annual conference of the African Evaluation Association (AfrEA). As an African American evaluator, my participation was first and foremost personally significant. It was equally a historically significant moment in global evaluation history. I took this opportunity to write a paper that reflected on evaluation approaches I personally believed had a major influence on the evaluation of schools and other educational institutions in the United States. Since the 1999 AfrEA conference, conversations in the evaluation literature and the American Evaluation Association about the role of culture and cultural context have resulted in additional personal reflections that are shared in this chapter.

I first take a historical look at selected program evaluation approaches and thoughts by a select group of evaluation theorists (in the case of some icons in the field) who have influenced my views as well as evaluative practices. The chapter considers the scholarly work of these individuals, the

An earlier version of this chapter was presented at the first annual meeting of the African Evaluation Association in Nairobi, Kenya, September 1999.

evaluation approaches they have articulated, and related discussions through my personal lens, which views cultural context and background as being central to the evaluation of programs designed to benefit those who are nonwhite and/or poor. It is my continuing belief that few evaluative approaches of the past (or for that matter the present) have seriously considered race, culture, poverty, or cultural context as anything more than "error variance." I remain firm in my conviction that program evaluation approaches can and should be more culturally responsive if we are to fully understand the effectiveness, benefits, and outcomes of programs designed to serve our less-powerful stakeholders. The chapter also discusses a few encouraging examples of emerging thinking about program evaluation approaches and standards offered by the evaluation community that may be conducive to achieving such objectives for this new millennium. One realistic remedy to advance the discourse and practice of educational evaluation is to increase the number of trained evaluators from racial and cultural groups that have typically been disenfranchised within the social fabric of the United States.

I begin with a discussion of Lee Cronbach's reflective and futuristic look (Cronbach and Associates, 1980) at the field of educational evaluation. I then turn to selected evaluation approaches from the first expansive thinking on American educational evaluation in the 1960s and 1970s, accompanied by the reflections of selected evaluation theorists about evaluation in the early 1990s. This is followed by a discussion of what I believe have been significant events in the past decade within the American Evaluation Association, as well as the personally significant Robert Stake Retirement Symposium, and the first AfrEA conference. All of these I have found to be personally encouraging for evaluative discourse and practice.

Tracks from History

A necessary beginning to this journey begins with a discussion of the historical influence of Lee Cronbach, Ralph Tyler, and other icons in the field on my notions of the role of culture in program evaluation.

Personal Reflections Informed by "Toward Reform in Program Evaluation." In a 1980 publication, *Toward Reform in Program Evaluation,* Lee Cronbach and associates reflected on what had transpired in the conceptualization, articulation, and practice of American program evaluation since the great evaluation proliferation of the 1960s. At the same time they suggested caution in applying evaluative approaches grounded in the American experience for other countries but recognized that new thinking about program evaluation would be necessary by the year 2000. Cronbach asserted: "Since we speak for the most part about evaluations of American social programs, our conclusions will not be equally appropriate outside of the United States. . . . Much of that we say would apply, with amendments, in other countries that have elaborate social programs. . . . As one moves away from the Western democratic tradition, however, the function or relevance of evaluation is likely to change. It also should be said that our thinking is in terms of the present, not of eternity. Our theses will have to be revised to fit the United States of the year 2000" (Cronbach and Associates 1980, p. 14).

These views, expressed by Cronbach more than twenty years ago, were instructive for my thinking and conversations at the AfrEA conference because they suggest that American thinking about program evaluation may have its limitations when applied without amendment in non-Western countries. Further, what was reasonable for evaluative thinking and practice then may not be for the new millennium. I believe that Cronbach was right on both counts.

Although the history of educational evaluation in the United States can be traced back to the 1890s, for many of us the father of program evaluation is considered to be Ralph Tyler (Worthen, Sanders, and Fitzpatrick, 1997). Tyler's eight-year study of thirty high schools in the 1930s gave important guidance to the systematic collection, analysis, and reporting of results for evaluative purposes. The approach simply sought to determine the extent to which the objectives of the educational program had indeed been achieved. This "objectives oriented" approach used instrumentation that measured predefined educational outcomes and thereby evaluated the extent to which the program achieved its desired outcomes. The guidelines that emerged from the eight-year study became a road map followed by many without interruption until the 1960s and is still evident in many educational evaluations conducted today.

Even though it is clear that Tyler's eight-year study "encouraged new thinking about the ends and means of education, . . . it did not inform policymakers about the effects of the programs it studied" (Cronbach and Associates, 1980, p. 29). It also failed to consider the relevance of social and cultural factors that may have been partly due to the inability of quantitative measurements to adequately represent these factors or their influence on the determination of program worth. Inclusion of key social and cultural factors was largely precluded since the interests of decision makers, as the primary stakeholders, were more highly honored than those of the less powerful stakeholders. Nevertheless, in some ways Tyler's objectives-oriented approach to program evaluation remained the evaluation law of the land until the 1960s because there were no sufficiently meaningful discussions of alternative ways to think about program evaluation.

Dawning of the Post-Tyler Era: 1960s and 1970s. Cronbach's 1963 paper on "Course Improvement Through Evaluation" was an early example of meaningful evaluation discourse and fueled a discussion on evaluation that prompted important elaborations on evaluation. In this paper, Cronbach "challenged evaluation strategists who were seeking a universally best instructional treatment and a one size fits all reform curriculum"

(Stake, 1991, p. 1). However, he also saw the paper as "an attempt to balance out the prevailing emphasis on summative evaluation" (Cronbach, 1982, p. xii). Nevertheless it was evident that the discourse on evaluation should be intensified.

A 1964 committee of the American Educational Research Association conducted a study of the need for standards in conducting evaluation studies and concluded that at that time standards were not needed; what was needed was expanded thinking and experimentation regarding evaluation (Stake, 1991). What emerged from these early discussions were Stake's "countenance of educational evaluation" (1967) and Scriven's "methodology of evaluation" (1967), which articulated the frameworks for distinguishing between summative and formative evaluation. Even though Stake would later discard the framework he proposed in the countenance paper in putting forth the notion of "responsive evaluation" (Scriven, 1991; Stake, 1991), the countenance paper was a conceptual breakthrough in thinking about program evaluation.

The limited view of program evaluation as an activity bounded by the Tylerian paradigm largely ignored those things that could not conveniently be put to quantitative measure. Consequently, the resulting evaluations that religiously followed this approach could only describe a program, the context in which it was designed and operated, and the outcomes for determining program worth to the extent that quantitative measures could do so. Even though there were admitted limitations with Stake's countenance approach, it did show that a rich description of the program and the context in which it functioned were critical to achieving more than superficial understanding. The countenance approach considers a program's antecedents (conditions precipitating the program), transactions (activities during implementation), and outcomes through the dense lens of what was intended by the program versus what was observed. Stake's approach for arriving at evaluative judgment, based on program standards, in some ways straddled the Tylerian fence. The identified program intents, transaction, and outcome dimensions of this approach could clearly be found within Tyler's objectives-oriented framework.

Incorporation of the conditions precipitating the program's creation and implementation offered the greatest potential for assessing the cultural and social nuances in programs designed for the benefit of stakeholders who had traditionally been disenfranchised in America. Further, Stake recognized that the unanticipated influences of a program merited our attention as well, in contrast to the Tylerian focus on preestablished program intents and designs. Unfortunately, this potential for richer description that could facilitate greater understanding was not realized at the time Stake proposed the countenance approach. There has been little evidence of cultural responsiveness in the work of those who used the countenance approach.

Scriven's elaborate distinction (1967) between formative and summative evaluation has also been a staple of many evaluators' diets. Cronbach

(1982) strongly criticized Scriven's definitions of formative and summative evaluation as convenient but in error. Even Scriven's later articulation of "goal free" evaluation (1972) was unacceptable to Cronbach (1982) because the approach excluded any interaction with program developers and proponents as a way to minimize evaluator bias. In fact, Cronbach asserted, "The evaluator who does not talk to persons having images of the program can only fantasize about what outcomes partisans hope for and skeptics fear, and how they expect these effects to develop. . . . The evaluator who avoids collegial relationships with program proponents escapes from certain forces that could bias him, but equally strong biases flow from his own commitments and preconceptions" (1982, p. 212).

Like Scriven's aforementioned works, Stufflebeam's Context Inputs Process Product (CIPP) approach (Stufflebeam and others, 1971) was also intended for the benefit of the manager or decision maker with a "strong decision oriented persuasion for the consideration of options and implications of administrative operations" (Stake, 1991, p. 71). CIPP's four types of evaluation (context, inputs, process, and product) were articulated to facilitate specific decisions to be made by program managers. An objectives-focused orientation is apparent in the CIPP approach, but its intents are clearly for those in authority. Nevertheless, it is context evaluation that may have held the most promise for contributing to a fuller understanding of programs designed for American racial minorities and the poor.

Stufflebeam and colleagues (1971) reported that the purpose of context evaluation "is to provide a rationale for determination of objectives for the system. It defines the environment, describes the desired and actual conditions pertaining to the environment, identifies unmet needs and unused opportunities and diagnoses the problems that prevent needs from being met and opportunities from being used" (p. 353).

Describing the context that influenced the need for a program is an important activity in evaluation. Description can facilitate evaluators' understanding of the environment in which the program must operate as well as the needs and expected benefits for stakeholders. The CIPP approach may have missed an opportunity to extend the concern for context beyond planning decisions, as well as the acknowledgment that the cultural nuances embedded in the experiences of racially and economically diverse groups are also important.

By 1978, Stake had moved beyond his disenchantment with his own countenance approach and articulated responsive evaluation. Responsive evaluation relies heavily on interviews and observations to achieve stakeholders' understanding of the evaluand and its perceived value or worth from multiple stakeholders' perspectives. I agree with Stake that "human observers are among our best instruments [and that] the evaluator should not rely only on his/her own powers of observation, judgment, and responding [but rather enlist] a platoon of students, teachers, and community leaders" (Stake, 1975). Anna Marie Madison (1992) and others (Chevalier,

Roark-Calnek, and Strahan, 1982; Wilcox, 1984) have implied that a responsive evaluation approach is one of the few that accepted culturally diverse factors as being central to "good" evaluation. Although some evaluators have been employing methods that can be viewed as culturally responsive, we still need to aggressively refine the methods we use in planning, collecting evaluative information, analyzing, interpreting, and making recommendations in a culturally responsive manner. I shall return to this topic after my review of how we got to where we are today.

The work of Guba and Lincoln (1981) expanded on Stake's notion of responsive evaluation in their articulation of naturalistic case studies. They made an important contribution by popularizing responsive evaluation from a theoretical to a practice orientation, but also by "pushing evaluators to pay attention to concepts of reality" (Stake, 1991, p. 83). In some ways the work of Stake, Guba, and Lincoln heeded Cronbach's 1960 contention that "what the evaluation field needs is a good social anthropologist" (as cited in Stake, 1991, p. 68). The work of Stake, and particularly his responsive evaluation approach, was a major influence on my thinking and practice as an evaluator. In some ways, I believe his work and that of Guba and Lincoln marked a transition in the thinking about evaluation, who should be served, and how to ensure meaningful inclusion of less powerful stakeholders. A few major events that occurred in the 1990s and particularly in the last few years of that decade were also personally instructive; I turn to them now.

Evaluation and Education: At Quarter Century. McLaughlin and Phillips published an edited volume in 1991, under the auspices of the National Society for the Study of Education, that presented reflections by selected evaluation theorists who had made major contributions to the field of evaluation. The volume included chapters by Tyler, Scriven, Stake, Alkin, Cook, Boruch, Eisner, Levin, Weis, House, and Stufflebeam. All presented thought-provoking discussions and analyses of their respective thinking on program evaluation over the preceding twenty-five years, reflections on the approaches they had been noted for, and the current state of affairs in program evaluation. It is not possible to discuss here the insights shared by all of these authors. However, it was the chapters by Tyler, Stake, and House that pushed my thinking about the need for program evaluation to be more responsive to cultural context in programs designed to serve American racial minorities and the poor.

Ralph Tyler's "General Statement on Program Evaluation" gave the perspective of someone with more than fifty years of evaluation experience and whose framework had dominated evaluation practice for many years. Even though I found limitations in the rigid objectives-oriented approach he prescribed, its importance to evaluation practice was undeniable. My problem with Tyler's approach was that it failed to address important variables such as cultural context that could not be adequately defined or described through quantitative measures but were nonetheless central to understanding a program and consequently determining its worth. However, in reading this particular chapter it was apparent that Tyler *had* acknowledged that one of the six major purposes of evaluation was to address those from "different populations." The six major purposes of program evaluation identified by Tyler (1991) were: "(1) to monitor present programs; (2) to select a better available program to replace one now in use that is deemed relatively ineffective; (3) to assist in developing a new program; (4) to identify the differential effects of the program with different populations of students or other clients; (5) to provide estimates of effects and costs in the catalogue of programs listed in consumer resource centers; and (6) to test the relevance and validity of the principles upon which the program is based" (p. 4).

These stated purposes do not deviate from what could be defined as an objectives-oriented evaluative framework, but the inclusion of considering the differential effects of the program with different clients was one that had not received paramount attention within this objectives-oriented framework.

Tyler (1991) presented a more extensive statement regarding "different populations": "Program evaluation is also used to identify [a program's] differential effects with different populations of students or clients where such differences as ethnic background, social class, education, and income of the family are thought to influence the effectiveness of the program" (p. 3).

It is important to consider the differential effects of a program when there are ethnic, educational, and socioeconomic differences—particularly if the program is designed to benefit those who have been traditionally disenfranchised. Yet Tyler's statement seems to be tentative about the importance of considering race, social class, education, and income within evaluation because they are merely "thought" to influence program effectiveness. There is mounting evidence that such considerations *are* of major importance in most of our American urban schools. Still, it was important that Tyler alluded to this as one of the purposes for which evaluations were being conducted.

Stake (1991) attempted to clarify the framework in the countenance paper and his dissatisfaction with the idea and how it had been used. He indicated that it was his intent to use standards data to identify levels of program quality to make independent judgments as to how well the program was doing and what it set out to do: "my standards data were background to help explain what people intended the program to be, and my judgment data were to indicate quality level of outcomes or discrepancies actually found" (p. 70). He believed that the countenance approach was useful for program description and determining congruence that made the case more "understandable," but the approach should not be used for determining program merit. In a reflective comment about his thinking at that time, he stated: "I held too much to the view that the important readers were people with research, administrative, and political authority. That was a mistake. I now see the important readers to be the immediate stakeholders of the immediate evaluand: teachers, local administrators, community leaders" (p. 75).

He found that his suggestion of a more responsive evaluation approach more appropriately increased understanding of a program on the basis of knowledge of its context through the experiential accounts of participants. Consequently he asserts that the design of an evaluation study should not be undertaken until the object of the evaluation is "well understood." Such understanding should be accomplished by using the "platoon" of human observers that Stake (1972) calls for in evaluation.

I state again what I have said elsewhere. It is critically important to ensure, or at least consider, the inclusion of evaluators and observers who share a "lived experience" with the cultural groups when evaluating programs that serve culturally diverse populations (Hood, 2001). I still maintain that central to the observation or the evaluation is *the meaning of what has been observed*. An evaluator's understanding of cultural context, when conducting an evaluation, is important. At the same time, I also resonate with Ernest House's articulation of the importance of social justice in evaluation.

The notion of social justice in evaluation characteristically means that the interests of all individuals and groups in a society are served but it places special emphasis on ensuring that the interests of the less powerful stakeholders are adequately addressed. House (1991) accurately pointed out that a "state of methodological grace" does not exist in evaluation; not all relevant interests are included in the planning and negotiation deliberations that determine policies and programs, and typically the less powerful and the poor are the ones excluded. He sees the social justice approach as being a "mechanism for evening out class barriers, instilling in persons a secure sense of self-worth, and empowering them to participate fully in the democratic process" (p. 242). Although House primarily identifies those who are excluded on the basis of social class, it is fair to say that in America these lines of exclusion are also drawn on race as well. It was expected that House would be criticized for taking such a position as being biased toward the disadvantaged; I could be equally criticized for holding such a view. Yet I concur with House's response to these critics: "It seems to me that making certain [that] interests of the disadvantaged are represented and seriously considered is not being biased, though it is certainly more egalitarian than most current practice" (p. 242). House would later extend his thinking regarding social justice and democracy in evaluation in the deliberative democratic evaluation approach (House and Howe, 1999).

A final comment on the McLaughlin and Phillips (1991) edited volume of educational evaluation at the quarter century: they provide an important benchmark in American educational evaluation. It may have not been a sufficient stimulus for innovative thinking in the work of evaluators for the remainder of the 1990s, but it encouraged evaluators to expand their thinking about issues of inclusion, democratic principles, and culture.

Encouraging Signs from the American Evaluation Association

In a two-year period (1993 and 1994) two addresses by presidents of the American Evaluation Association (AEA) and publication of the revised Program Evaluation Standards (1994, second edition) afforded insights into the educational evaluation community's attempt to broaden its views about how evaluations should be conducted.

In 1993, AEA President David Fetterman articulated the "empowerment evaluation" approach in his presidential address at the association's annual meeting. Empowerment evaluation was described as an approach that could be used as a vehicle of evaluation in the form of training, facilitation, advocacy, illumination, or liberation (Fetterman, 1994). At its core, empowerment evaluation uses "concepts and techniques to foster improvement and self determination" (Mertens, 1997, p. 235). The notion of empowerment as being a vehicle of self-determination for less powerful stakeholders is indeed commendable, and the examples Fetterman offered were reflective of this objective. Nevertheless, the model was criticized by Stufflebeam (1994) as an exercise in public relations rather than an evaluation. It was also suggested that the empowerment evaluation approach did not go far enough because it did not "explicitly address the issues of power related to sexism, racism, or oppression of people with disabilities" (Whitmore, 1996, as cited in Mertens, 1997). Empowerment evaluation may have opened up new possibilities in the thinking and practice of evaluation, but it was too early to determine if the concept would endure (Patton, 1994).

The following year another AEA president offered an aggressive proposition for evaluators—in the form of *multicultural validity*. At the 1994 AEA conference, Karen Kirkhart's presidential address proposed what was surely a more direct assault on the lack of attention to culture in program evaluation than had been the case for any previous AEA president (at least to this author's knowledge), asserting that "multicultural validity. . . . be conceptualized as a central dimension of validity, treated with the same respect, routinization, and scrutiny as other dimensions; that is, it should be a visible focus of concern in evaluation theory, methodology, practice and meta-evaluation" (Kirkhart, 1995, p. 1).

Clearly, the proposition that multicultural validity should be a central concern in program evaluation suggested that generally program evaluators had not been sensitive to this concern. Consequently, it was quite likely that much of evaluative work had not included multicultural perspectives in the evaluations. Even if lip service had been given to the notion of culturally diverse perspectives, it was questionable whether these views were presented accurately, soundly, and appropriately. Thus, I do concur with Kirkhart that it is important that we as evaluators consider "multicultural validity as a unifying construct whose thoughtful examination can help to improve methodology and raise our individual awareness of the complexity of the issues. Scholarly treatment of this topic will, hopefully, lay the groundwork for a more integrated response to cultural diversity in our profession" (Kirkhart, 1995, p. 8).

I was encouraged by Kirkhart's AEA presidential address. It unequivocally brought the issue of culture before the members of the American Evaluation Association. Further, there was similar evidence regarding the importance of culture in evaluation found in the publication of the revised program evaluation standards (PES) the same year.

The utility standards suggest that evaluators be required to "acquaint themselves with their audience, define the audiences clearly, ascertain audience's information needs, plan evaluations to respond to these needs, and report the relevant information clearly and in a timely fashion" (Joint Committee on Standards for Educational Evaluation, 1994, p. 5). One way to achieve this objective is to identify stakeholders. The standards suggest (1) that it is necessary to include "less powerful groups or individuals as stakeholders, such as racial, cultural, or language minority groups"; (2) determining how the respective stakeholders view the evaluation's importance, how they would like to use the results, and what information will be particularly useful; and (3) including the clients and stakeholders in designing and conducting the evaluation. It should be no surprise that I believe such steps would contribute to our making program evaluation more culturally responsive. However, it was interesting that the standards did not consider the importance of less powerful stakeholders assisting the evaluator in interpreting an evaluation's results.

An evaluator's credibility is probably one of the most critical criteria for selecting who should conduct an evaluation. The U.S. PES criteria for evaluator credibility are that (1) the evaluator should be trustworthy and competent to conduct the evaluation, (2) the evaluator should be knowledgeable of the social and political forces affecting the less powerful stakeholders and use this information in designing and conducting the evaluation, and (3) the work plan and composition of the evaluation team are responsive to key stakeholders. These are fine guidelines, and clearly these standards resonate with what would be expected of a culturally responsive evaluator as well. Unfortunately, it is rare that we find evidence that these standards for evaluator credibility have been implemented or seriously considered in the evaluation of our urban schools. Yet a more expanded view of an evaluator's credibility could be considered when selecting an evaluator to evaluate a program serving a racial minority group.

Grace (1992) offered another perspective on evaluator credibility when working with African American communities that could also apply to other groups of color. She indicates that "in many cultures the age, race, sex, and credentials of the evaluators may have a significant impact on the evaluation process. . . . [In the case of African Americans]—all things being equal—the most influential and respected members of the evaluation team are likely to be older individuals with academic credentials related to their expertise as evaluators" (p. 63).

It seems only reasonable and appropriate that every effort should be made to include external evaluators who have a shared, lived experience when evaluating programs in racial minority communities. Yet racial similarity should not be the only requirement considered beyond competency. It may also be appropriate to follow Grace's recommendation to interview potential evaluators using questions designed to tap culturally relevant knowledge, attitudes, and skills. The evaluator's answers to these questions may be a good indication of a candidate's suitability for the job as an evaluator, which is something for us to think about.

The previously noted AEA presidential addresses and inclusive wording of the standards call for evaluators to do more than be sensitive to issues of cultural diversity and less powerful stakeholders. They call for taking action in their evaluation research and practice. I am encouraged that major steps have been taken by the AEA to bring the issues of culture and cultural context into its mainstream conversation over the past few years. AEA's undertaking of the Building Diversity Initiative (funded by the Kellogg Foundation), establishment of a diversity committee as an AEA standing committee, and more recently a "cultural reading" of the program evaluation standards by the diversity committee are significant and positive steps. Yet this journey is merely beginning.

I turn now to another personally significant event that furthered my thinking about the role of culture and cultural context in evaluation: the retirement symposium for Robert Stake in 1998.

Robert E. Stake Retirement Symposium

The retirement symposium for Robert Stake in May 1998 at the University of Illinois at Urbana-Champaign was another positive sign that contributed to elevating the discussion about evaluation—where we had been, where we were, and where we might need to go as evaluators. More than 250 people gathered at this two-day symposium in Urbana, Illinois, with thirty or more papers presented on many aspects of program evaluation. Among the presenters were Lee Cronbach, Gene Glass, Jennifer Greene, Ernest House, Richard Jaeger, Les Lean, James Sanders, Michael Scriven, and Nick Smith. It is not possible to adequately capture the significance of the dialogue and exchange that occurred over those two days at the University of Illinois. The papers were but the starting point for the discussions that would ensue during the sessions, breaks, dinners, and social hours. This stellar group of scholars who had contributed much to educational measurement and program evaluation gave me an opportunity to test and advance my ideas about program evaluation. Although I took part in many discussions over the course of those two days, it was Michael Scriven's paper on the meaning of bias that pushed my thinking.

At the Stake symposium, I presented a paper entitled "Responsive Evaluation Amistad Style: Perspectives of One African American Evaluator" (Hood, 1998). In it I asserted that too many evaluations in American urban schools failed to address culture as an important consideration in the design, data collection, analysis, and interpretation of evaluative data. I suggested that if we extended Stake's thinking on responsive evaluation, it was possible to design and implement evaluations that were more culturally responsive and would begin to address the construct of multicultural validity in evaluation as proposed by Kirkhart (1995). I argued that one possible explanation as to why we as evaluators were unable to achieve such an objective was because there were too few trained evaluators with lived experience among American racial minorities or the poor. Consequently, more often than not, too many evaluators are limited in their ability to understand cultural nuances that could influence the evaluation process. I asserted that more evaluators who shared a lived experience with those who have been traditionally disenfranchised in the American educational system could make a valuable contribution to evaluative thinking and practice. Scriven (1998) only partly agreed; I sensed that his view was shared by others.

Scriven (1998) discussed his views on bias within the context of evaluation by first suggesting that bias in "the evaluative context is itself an evaluative term, referring to the disposition to avoidable error and its presence is then by definition undesirable" (p. 15). Few could argue against the point that bias should not be found in our practice as evaluators. It was Scriven's later comments that were personally provocative: "Stafford Hood reminded us yesterday, there are potential, indeed probable elements of racial bias in our practice not thoroughly explored and dealt with yet. We still have a job to do in the elimination of bias itself. But this is not job number one. Job number one is getting the bias out of action and practice" (p. 18).

This task must be done, but it appears to overlook my argument for more trained evaluators from diverse racial groups who have largely been absent in the evaluation community.

Should we rethink our current approaches to educational evaluation? Of course. But our greatest need does not lie exclusively there. It lies as well with *who* does the thinking. If one wants to change the game, one can change the rules or one can change the players. My argument is that we have an adequate set of rules, but they are in desperate need of an overhaul, to guide our conduct in educational evaluation. Moreover, we urgently need an infusion of new players. A variety of historical lessons suggest the cast of actors profoundly affects not only the outcome of the activity but the very nature of the activity itself. Consider the decision of the Roman Catholic Church in the 1960s to "throw open its windows" (Tolson, 1992). The church already had a plethora of papal pronouncements on the need to honor the disenfranchised. It did not need new rules or a rethinking of its old rules so much as it needed new people to renew and implement what it already had. To that end, the pope appointed dozens of bishops and cardinals of color. The issues and perspectives these newly enfranchised prelates brought to the social action of the church profoundly affected the course of its recent history.

I believe the challenge in American and international evaluation during this new millennium is to include new players in evaluative discourse and practice. I am encouraged by the knowledge that there a few developing young evaluators from American racial minority groups who are readying themselves to make important contributions to the field of evaluation. It is my hope that the creation of the African Evaluation Association and the national evaluation associations that have sprung up in other African countries will be the opportunity for new evaluation players as well. The recent African evaluation guidelines that have emerged from AfrEA (Nairobi M&E Network and others, 2002) may also be instructive as the American evaluation community undertakes its upcoming revision of the program evaluation standards.

African Evaluation Guidelines

Creation of the AfrEA and its first annual conference in Nairobi, Kenya (September 1999), was a critically important opportunity for the three hundred participants (representing thirty-five countries) to think anew about evaluation standards, theory, and practice in the African and global evaluation community. It was a great personal and professional honor to be one of the participants at this inaugural moment in evaluation history, and I would say the birth of AfrEA has already yielded considerable fruit. One example is the increasing number of national evaluation associations in African countries since 1999; another is the African evaluation guidelines (Nairobi M&E Network and others, 2002).

As I thought about the appropriateness of the U.S. program evaluation standards for use in African countries before, during, and after the 1999 AfrEA conference, it was apparent that there were those who believed the Western educational evaluation standards should be adopted in toto. In some ways, this was reminiscent of a Western colonial mentality that "we know best" what African educational systems and evaluators need. I believed then, and now, that it would be wrong to accept evaluative standards to guide evaluative practices that have seemingly been effective in the United States because it assumes that American evaluation models are directly applicable. It further assumes that Western evaluators already know what African evaluators need. I have argued that most American evaluation models have not been responsive to less powerful stakeholders in America who are typically members of racial minorities and/or poor. So why should one assume that American evaluators know what is needed in the context of African educational evaluation?

One of the major plenary session discussions at the 1999 AfrEA conference addressed the U.S. program evaluation standards. A modified version of a paper by Russon and Patel (1998) proposed certain changes to the U.S. program evaluation standards (U.S. PES) and served as the starting point of conversation at this plenary session. The questions posed for discussion to the AfrEA participants were simply: Should the U.S. PES be adopted without modification for application in Africa? Should a set of African evaluation standards be developed by African countries from scratch? Or should the U.S. PES be modified and studied to determine their utility for African evaluation? I must admit that my position was that AfrEA and its member national evaluation associations should start anew and develop a set of evaluation guidelines by them, for them, and to be used by any evaluator evaluating programs in African countries. There were those who agreed with my thinking, but I do understand why the compromise position to modify the U.S. PES and study their utility was an appropriate starting point.

The modifications of the thirty U.S. standards were published in 2002 as the African Evaluation Guidelines; they were the result of a series of workshops, meetings, and the 1999 AfrEA inaugural conference. Thus far thirteen of the thirty U.S. standards have been modified for inclusion in the African evaluation guidelines to "make them more readily applicable to current African cultural, social and political realities. . . . [The] political and cultural considerations emerged as major driving forces behind the necessary modifications" (Nairobi M&E Network and others, 2002, p. 488). Specifically, cultural considerations were of critical importance in modifying the U.S. standards pertaining to property, "formal agreements" (P2), "rights of human subjects" (P3), and "human interactions" (P4).

One example is particularly illustrative of the challenge and necessity of modifying U.S. PES so that they are responsive to African cultural considerations. In the United States, development, negotiation, or monitoring of "written" formal agreements is governed by some form of "written" law. In nearly all cases, what has been written takes precedence over what has not been written. However, the African evaluation guidelines made it clear that when addressing cultural considerations "law is not always more important than tradition or custom" (Nairobi M&E Network and others, 2002, p. 485). This consideration should also not be ignored as the American Evaluation Association's diversity committee continues its "cultural reading" of the U.S. PES and as the Joint Committee on Standards for Educational Evaluation begins its process to revise the standards. In fact, it may be highly advisable that those who are involved in the upcoming process to "revise" the U.S. PES pay close attention to the African evaluation guidelines and give some of them careful consideration for adoption.

Earlier in this chapter, I asserted my agreement with Stake that the construct of *understanding* is important in the evaluation process. It is also a critical consideration in our discussions and deliberation within the evaluation community. For example, Scriven's response to my thoughts at the Stake retirement symposium advised that evaluators should search their souls for bias that may impede their ability to fairly evaluate a program.

Good idea and a good start, but not the one I was advancing. It was also the case that in my conversation with other distinguished attendees at this symposium, they too thought I was addressing the policies of affirmative action, which, again, is an important issue but not to the point. Some have even viewed my position regarding making evaluation (see Hood, 2001) and assessments (see Hood, 1999) more culturally responsive as an effort to diminish the importance of statistical methods, rather than to strike an equitable balance (when appropriate) between quantitative and qualitative approaches. On the contrary, I appreciate the place of quantitative data in our evaluations.

I do not diminish the importance of people's perceptions and interpretations of the views I express. I cannot tell them what they should think or do as a consequence of what I have said. If members of the evaluation family see fit to reconsider their behaviors as a consequence of my arguments, that is good. But that is not my main message about culturally responsive evaluation—at least, from the perspective of this African American evaluator. I am trying to say more, much more. I am saying that evaluators of color must be at the table when the evaluation family eats its meals and engages in conversation about family matters. We have something to say about the family's decisions, how its resources are distributed, and how the family's well-being is evaluated. Our evaluation family's membership must be broadened and renewed. Until that message is honored, culturally responsive evaluation will not achieve its promise.

Ralph Tyler had it right. Properly used with a culturally responsive approach, the good work of Tyler, Stake, and Stufflebeam permits midcourse corrections in evaluation. It permits feedback to the decision makers for change. Evaluations, correctly done, bring resources rather than merely expend them. African, South American, and other non-U.S. and Western European countries must be concerned with economic development in all of their evaluation activities. As a consequence, one should be open to all modes of inquiry, be they large-scale data analysis or single-site case studies. What is at the heart of any evaluation counsel is competence and sensitivity; we seek evaluators who know the range of approaches available and who are able to listen in a culturally responsive and responsible manner.

Epilogue

This chapter has offered selected reflections and snapshots that have informed my thinking in my personal journey to understand the role of culture in program evaluation. It will be nothing less than a lifelong endeavor— as it should be. I can find no logical explanation as to why our evaluations should not be culturally responsive or why we should not behave in culturally responsible ways in our work as evaluators. Culturally responsive and responsible evaluations are not new phenomena. In fact, evidence continues to emerge that African American educational evaluators employed culturally responsive and responsible strategies in their evaluation of segregated schools in the South because it was the socially responsible thing to do (Hood, 2001). It still is.

Recent efforts by the American Evaluation Association, the African Evaluation Association, and a slow but steadily growing contingent within the evaluation community encourage some of us to be cautiously optimistic about the contributions we can make as evaluators when we work in communities that have been and continue to be disenfranchised. Our efforts to address issues of culture and cultural context in the upcoming process to revise the program evaluation standards may be our opportunity to "forge a new morality, to create the principles on which a new world will be built" (Baldwin, 1972, p. 90).

References

Baldwin, J. *No Name in the Street*. New York: Dial Press, 1972.

Chevalier, Z. W., Roark-Calnek, S., and Strahan, D. B. "Responsive Evaluation of an Indian Heritage Studies Program: Analyzing Boundary Definition in a Suburban School Context." Paper presented at the annual meeting of the American Educational Research Association, New York City, Mar. 1982.

Cronbach, L. J. *Designing Evaluations of Educational and Social Programs*. San Francisco: Jossey-Bass, 1982.

Cronbach, L. J., and Associates. *Toward Reform of Program Evaluation*. San Francisco: Jossey-Bass, 1980.

Fetterman, D. M. "Empowerment Evaluation." *Evaluation Practice,* 1994, *15*(1), 1–15.

Grace, C. A. "Practical Considerations for Program Professionals and Evaluators Working with African American Communities." In M. A. Orlandi (ed.), *Cultural Competence for Evaluators: A Guide for Alcohol and Other Drug Abuse Prevention with Practitioners Working with Ethnic/Racial Communities*. Rockville, Md.: U.S. Department of Health and Human Services, 1992.

Guba, E. G., and Lincoln, Y. S. *Effective Evaluation*. San Francisco: Jossey-Bass, 1981.

Hood, S. "Responsive Evaluation Amistad Style: Perspectives of One African American Evaluator." In R. Sullivan (ed.), *Proceedings of the Stake Symposium on Educational Evaluation*. Champaign, Ill.: University of Illinois at Urbana-Champaign, 1998.

Hood, S. "Assessment in the Context of Culture and Pedagogy: A Collaborative Effort, a Meaningful Goal." *Journal of Negro Education,* 1999, *67*(3), 184–186.

Hood, S. "Nobody Knows My Name: In Praise of African American Evaluators Who Were Responsive." In J. Greene and T. Abma (eds.), *Responsive Evaluation: Roots and Wings*. New Directions for Evaluation, no. 92. San Francisco: Jossey-Bass, 2001.

House, E. *Educational Policy Analysis Archives*. 1991.

House, E. R., and Howe, K. R. *Values in Evaluation and Social Research*. Thousand Oaks, Calif.: Sage, 1999.

Joint Committee on Standards for Educational Evaluation. *The Program Evaluation Standards*. (2nd ed.) Thousand Oaks, Calif.: Sage, 1994.

Kirkhart, K. E. "Seeking Multicultural Validity: A Postcard from the Road." *Evaluation Practice,* 1995, *16*(1), 1–12.

Madison, A. M. (ed.). *Minority Issues in Program Evaluation*. New Directions for Program Evaluation, no. 53. San Francisco: Jossey-Bass, 1992.

McLaughlin, M. W., and Phillips, D. C. *Evaluation: At Quarter Century*. Chicago: University of Chicago Press, 1991.

Mertens, D. M. *Research Methods in Education and Psychology: Integrating Diversity with Quantitative and Qualitative Approaches.* Thousand Oaks, Calif.: Sage, 1997.

Nairobi M&E Network, and others. "The African Evaluation Guidelines 2002: A Checklist to Assist in Planning Evaluations, Negotiating Clear Contracts, Reviewing Progress, and Ensuring Adequate Completion of an Evaluation." *Evaluation and Program Planning,* 2002, *25,* 481–492.

Patton, M. Q. "Developmental Evaluation." *Evaluation Practice,* 1994, *15*(3), 311–320.

Russon, C., and Patel, M. "Appropriateness of the Program Evaluation Standards for Use in Africa." Paper presented to the African Evaluation Association, 1998.

Scriven, M. "The Methodology of Evaluation." In R. Stake (ed.), *Perspectives of Curriculum Evaluation.* Skokie, Ill.: Rand McNally, 1967.

Scriven, M. "Pros and Cons About Goal-Free Evaluation." *Evaluation Comment,* 1972, *3,* 1–7.

Scriven, M. *Evaluation Thesaurus.* (4th ed.) Thousand Oaks, Calif.: Sage, 1991.

Scriven, M. "The Meaning of Bias." In R. Davis (ed.), *The Proceedings of the Stake Symposium on Educational Evaluation.* Champaign, IL: University of Illinois at Urbana-Champaign, 1998.

Stake, R. E. "The Countenance of Educational Evaluation." *Teachers College Record,* Apr. 1967, *68,* 523–540.

Stake, R. E. *Responsive Evaluation.* 1972. (ED 075–187)

Stake, R. E. "Program Evaluation, Particularly Responsive Evaluation." Paper presented at a conference on new trends in evaluation, Goteborg, Sweden, Oct. 1975.

Stake, R. E. "Retrospective on 'The Countenance of Educational Evaluation.'" In M. W. McLaughlin and D. C. Phillips (eds.), *Evaluation: At Quarter Century.* (Ninetieth Yearbook of the National Society for the Study of Education). Chicago: University of Chicago Press, 1991.

Stufflebeam, D. L. "Empowerment Evaluation, Objectivist Evaluation, and Evaluation Standards: Where the Future of Evaluation Should Not Go and Where It Needs to Go." *Evaluation Practice,* 1994, *15*(3), 321–338.

Stufflebeam, D. L., and others. *Educational Evaluation and Decision Making.* Itasca, Ill.: Peacock, 1971.

Tolson, J. *Pilgrim in the Ruins.* New York: Simon & Schuster, 1992.

Tyler, R. W. "General Statement on Program Evaluation." In M. W. McLaughlin and D. C. Phillips (eds.), *Evaluation: At Quarter Century.* Chicago: University of Chicago Press, 1991.

Wilcox, T. "Evaluating Programs for Native Students: A Responsive Strategy." Paper presented at the Mokakit Indian Education Research Association's International Conference, London, Ontario, Canada, July 1984.

Worthen, B., Sanders, J. R., and Fitzpatrick, J. L. *Program Evaluation: Alternative Approaches and Practical Guidelines.* White Plains, N.Y.: Longman, 1997.

STAFFORD HOOD is an associate division director and associate professor of counseling/counseling psychology in the Division of Psychology in Education at Arizona State University. He is the founding codirector of an annual national conference on the relevance of assessment in culture in evaluation.

3

Culturally competent evaluation in Indian Country requires an understanding of the rich diversity of tribal peoples and the importance of self-determination and sovereignty. If an evaluation can be embedded within an indigenous framework, it is more responsive to tribal ethics and values. An indigenous orientation to evaluation suggests methodological approaches, a partnership between the evaluator and the program, and reciprocity.

Culturally Competent Evaluation in Indian Country

Joan LaFrance

Given the rich tapestry of tribal cultures in the United States, it is presumptuous to assume that any evaluator, whether an Alaskan Native or a member of an American Indian tribe (or a non-Indian), can understand the culture of every group. Rather than trying to master multiple cultural specificities, the goal of a competent evaluator, especially in Indian Country, should be to actively seek cultural grounding through the ongoing processes of appreciating the role of tribal sovereignty, seeking knowledge of the particular community, building relationships, and reflecting on methodological practices. This article is an opportunity for discourse and reflection on these many levels. It discusses the importance of understanding the implications of sovereignty when working in Indian Country, the significance of an emerging indigenous framework for evaluation, Indian self-determination in setting the research and evaluation agenda, and finally particular methodological approaches I find useful in my evaluation practice.

For this discussion, I use the term *Indian Country* to describe the collection of tribal nations and Alaskan native communities that occupy a shared homeland and live in culturally bounded communities. The term *indigenous* refers to the first native residents of lands that have been taken over by outsider populations—specifically, Indian tribes and Alaskan Natives in North and South America, and the Pacific.

An early draft of sections of this chapter was presented at the AEA annual meeting in 2001. The chapter also draws from contributions to "Promoting Culturally Reliable and Valid Evaluation Practice," a chapter to appear in an edition of *Evaluation and Society* that I coauthored with Sharon Nelson-Barber, Elise Trumbull, and Sofia Aburto of WestEd.

Understanding Sovereignty

Few Americans fully appreciate the political status of American Indians and Alaskan Natives. In Indian Country, sovereignty expresses recognition of and respect for tribal governance and nationhood. Treaties between tribes and the United States established a unique federal-tribal relationship. This relationship is also recognized in numerous executive orders and acts of Congress. Programs operating on Indian reservations operate within a civil structure unfamiliar to most Americans. Tribes are governmental units separate from state and local governments. In many tribes, the governing bodies include a general council, composed of all tribal citizens age eighteen and above, and an elected business council, which is usually called the tribal council. Other tribes have more traditional forms of governments based on historical leadership patterns. Recent federal laws have encouraged tribal self-determination and self-governance. As a result, many tribes now operate their own educational, health, and welfare programs through funding relationships with the federal government.

More than thirty years ago, a well-known husband-and-wife anthropologist team noted that their profession had studied American Indians more than any other group in the world (Swisher, 1993). This intensive scrutiny from the outside has been problematic to many American Indian people, whose tribes and families have suffered from a long history of intrusive studies that have built the reputations of anthropologists and other researchers but brought little more than loss of cultural ownership and exploitation to Indian people. The research studies often depicted Indians in a naïve or negative light. Trimble's review (1977) of articles on Indian educational research found that most of the literature concentrated on problems centered around the investigator's interest, and not those of the tribal people from whom the data were obtained. Because evaluation draws on methods of anthropology, among other social sciences, evaluation in Indian Country may suffer from a similar legacy.

With the growing emphasis on self-determination, it is not surprising that some tribal governments are establishing formal processes to protect themselves from the abuses of research. Although program evaluation is somewhat different in that it seeks to understand and contribute to programs within the context of the community, the collective tribal history with research has contributed to a general distrust of outsiders who come to study, ask questions, and publish their findings (Crazy Bull, 1997). Evaluators need to learn whether official approval is needed to conduct the evaluation, and evaluators must be sensitive to particular tribal processes involved in working with research committees. Tribal sovereignty also fuels concern about access to data and uses of evaluation information. Since tribes are continuously engaged in struggles to protect their rights, they are hesitant to have evaluation findings reflect negatively on the social, economic, or political goals of the community.

Because tribal governments are much smaller than local and state governments, programs operating under tribal authority are much more closely connected to local political structures than are most other publicly funded programs. As a result, programs operating under tribal governing structures tend to be more susceptible to social and political forces at work in a community. As such, they have a greater obligation to be responsive to community priorities and concerns. Evaluation can make an important contribution to developing responsive and effective programs in tribal communities. The challenges for culturally competent evaluators in Indian Country are to move past ingrained reticence toward research and instead actively engage the key stakeholders in creating the knowledge needed to deliver effective services.

Evaluation can become even more responsive to tribal programs if it is couched within indigenous "ways of knowing" and knowledge creation. The National Science Foundation (NSF) has funded a project of the American Indian Higher Education Consortium (AIHEC) to develop an "indigenous framework" for evaluation. The framework will guide a training curriculum for educators in Indian Country. AIHEC is undertaking this work because more Indian communities are developing and implementing new strategies for improving the educational attainment of their youth that draw from traditional values and culture. In so doing, it is urgent to establish new evaluation processes that are broad enough to accommodate and value different ways of knowing, build ownership and a sense of community within groups of Indian educators, and efficiently contribute to development of high-quality and sustainable Indian and Alaskan native education programs. Building an indigenous evaluation framework will contribute to the national evaluation discourse through inclusion of indigenous epistemologies—ways of knowing—that are not typically included in standard Western evaluation models. By supporting incorporation of indigenous epistemologies into Western evaluation practice, the field will be more responsive to the educational interventions that are using traditional and cultural approaches.

The Case for an Indigenous Evaluation Framework

In her discussion of decolonializing research in indigenous communities, Smith (1999) advocates the importance of creating designs that ensure validity and reliability by being based on community values and indigenous ways of knowing. Deloria (1999) argues that there is a need to make a concerted effort to gather traditional tribal wisdom into a coherent body of knowledge: "I believe firmly that tribal ways represent a complete and logical alternative to Western science. If tribal wisdom is to be seen as a valid intellectual discipline, it will be because it can be articulated in a wide variety of expository forms and not simply in the language and concepts that tribal elders have always used" (p. 66). Garroutte (2003) argues that indigenous ways of knowing can find a place in the academy only if those with access to the academy make it a safe place for indigenous knowledge. Evaluation is a good candidate for building this bridge. Though based on Western research models, evaluation, as Weiss (1998) notes, is a practical craft; evaluators engage in the craft to contribute to program quality. With their nod toward practicality, evaluators can take liberties to explore cultural epistemologies that differ from those taught in the academy if such exploration contributes to the validity and usefulness of evaluation in the context of program operations. Those evaluators who belong to the academy should also be able to bring the fruits of their explorations into the academic discourse. Consequently, evaluators who learn how to practice in a culturally competent framework have the potential for changing not only the field of evaluation but also conversations on knowledge creation, its components, and its ramifications. For this reason, I would like to share some of our emerging thoughts about an indigenous framework for evaluation.

Elements in an Indigenous Framework

There is a growing discussion among indigenous scientists and evaluation experts about native or indigenous approaches to knowledge generation that are in contrast to Western ways of knowing. At a recent AEA conference, Hayley Govina (2002) described how her Maori values required that in her culture "evidence" must be "trust-based" and grow out of mutual understanding and relationship. She contrasted this Maori "valued knowledge" approach with a Western research model that is "evidence based" and capable of selecting out factors and looking at them in isolation. At the same AEA conference, Andrea Johnston (2002) described how Western evaluation logic models are linear and interested in isolated domains such as indicators or factors. In her Ojibwe world, knowledge is holistic, and the focus is on how the spheres (of factors) overlap to produce growth. In his book on native science, Greg Cajete (2000) contrasts the opposing cosmologies of Western culture, where a God is apart from the earth and man is given dominion over the material world, and the indigenous belief that man comes from the earth and all elements of the world are equal. In his work, Cajete defines models, causality, interpretation, and explanation in ways that go beyond objective measurement but honor the importance of direct experience, interconnectedness, relationship, holism, and value.

Indigenous knowledge values holistic thinking (Cajete, 2000; Christensen, 2002), which contrasts with the linear and hierarchical thinking that characterizes much of Western evaluation practice. Cajete also describes the profound "sense of place" woven throughout native thought. This strong connection to place, location, and community is in sharp contrast to modern American values of mobility and individualization—values that often define "success" in contemporary America.

Cajete further describes how Indian people experience nature as part of themselves and themselves as part of nature, adding that "this is the ultimate form of being 'indigenous' and forms the basis for a fully internalized bonding with that place" (p. 187). Although history of contact with Europeans has altered indigenous connections to their original lands, the sense of place is still a deeply held value. Despite their outward appearance of poverty and limited development, reservations are cherished homelands. Tribes invest energy and resources to regain lost land and develop opportunities on the reservations. For many programs operating on reservations, an important criterion of success is their contribution to the larger tribal goals of restoration and preservation.

Indian tribes also possess a strong sense of community. This is found in many tribal languages, in which the name for the tribe translates into English as "the people," as is the case for the *Dené* (Navajo), or the *Anishinabe* (Chippewa or Ojibwe) "spontaneously created people. Original tribal names distinguished the uniqueness of the group in relation to the rest of the world" (Deloria, 1994). Maintenance of the tribal community is an important criterion of successful programs and services in Indian Country.

Christensen (2002) describes the values of an elder epistemology, noting that "with its emphasis on oral skills it is an important intellectual construct, yet it is neither practiced nor even deemed relevant in the academic community" (p. 5). Drawing from the example of elder teaching, Christensen describes the role of respect, reciprocity, and relationship. In practice these three R's suggest an approach to evaluation that understands the tribal context, contributes knowledge and builds capacity in the community, and is practiced by evaluators who value building strong relationships with those involved in the evaluation. Elder teaching is based on a democratic value of give and take, equality, and participation. Smith (1999) reinforces this ethic of respect: "From the indigenous perspectives ethical codes of conduct serve partly the same purpose as the protocols which govern our relationships with each other and with the environment. The term 'respect' is consistently used by indigenous peoples to underscore the significance of our relationships and humanity. Through respect the place of everyone and everything in the universe is kept in balance and harmony" (p. 120).

Smith also describes an indigenous research agenda in which the very naming of the research agenda denotes self-determination. She writes, "What researchers may call methodology, for example, Maori researchers in New Zealand call Kaupapa Maori research or Maori-centered research. Such naming accords indigenous values, attitudes and practices a privileged, central position rather than obscuring them under Westernized labels such as 'collaborative research'" (p. 125). This suggests that as indigenous people move into evaluating their programs, they take charge of their own agenda; name their own evaluation processes; and use the methodologies that fit within their framing of place, community, values, and culture.

Reflections on Evaluation Methodology

In a country that values mobility, competitiveness, and progress, the Indian values for preservation, continuity, and community seem somewhat out of place. Yet it is these more conservative values that underlie many of the programs and projects that are subject to outside evaluations. Failure to understand such values, or imposing more mainstream assumptions upon the definitions of successful outcomes, results in evaluations that fail to contribute to tribal goals and program expectations. Understanding the importance of the values and the elements emerging in the indigenous framing of evaluation, as well as my experience doing evaluation in Indian Country, suggests a number of methodological considerations: the importance of formative evaluation, the value of building conceptual models, the importance of participatory processes and building evaluation capacity, issues in using qualitative and quantitative methods, and challenges in doing comparative research.

Importance of Formative Evaluation. The more conservative values of preservation and restoration operating on Indian reservations suggest that tribal programs need to be evaluated within their own context. The major evaluation questions become formative and tribe-specific ("How can we improve our service delivery?" or "What have we learned from this program or project?"). The view is inward; questions that imply comparison with populations outside the tribal community are less relevant to a community that is focused on its own growth and development. I found this to be true when researching evaluation issues in tribal schools in the 1980s. Reacting to a national evaluation driven by political forces in Congress against the tribal movement to control their own schools, the Senate commissioned a study of tribally controlled schools. The study specifically requested that these schools be matched with public schools serving students on the same reservation that also had a tribal school. The schools were compared on achievement, attendance, and per-pupil costs. Although the study failed to yield much of value for the political forces driving it, it definitely was not useful for administrators and staff in tribal schools. My research (LaFrance, 1990) found that the evaluation interests of tribal school personnel centered on "within school" concerns. They were interested in students doing well over their time in the school and whether they were developing a good sense of self-esteem. They wanted to know if the curriculum was meeting its objectives. They did value learning how their school compared to others; however, this question was of secondary importance and one that would not drive policy decisions.

To ensure sharing formative knowledge, I have arranged to regularly debrief program directors regarding initial evaluation findings. Since tribal institutions are small, the director or principal investigator is often the single person coping with delivery of social services or educational programs. Unlike administrators who work in larger institutions, she does not have colleagues with whom to share concerns or learn about resources. Regular evaluation debriefings bring to her another person to whom she can talk about the issues encountered in operating the project. The evaluator becomes a resource for testing ideas or seeking advice. Although this might step outside the boundaries of evaluation, it is an important value-added contribution in resource-strapped communities (LaFrance, 2002b).

Building the Conceptual Picture. Given the inward orientation and the importance of understanding the assumptions and values driving programs operating on Indian reservations, I find it useful to work with stakeholders to articulate a theory of change (Weiss, 1998) prior to developing the evaluation plan. This is done in a facilitated workshop. The first objective of the workshop is to explicate the underlying assumptions guiding the program. All of the workshop participants have an opportunity to discuss what they do. Since everyone has tasks and activities, all are equally included in the discussion. Once activities are mapped out, the workshop participants are asked what will change as a result of the activities, or what their assumptions for change are. This is a much deeper question and leads to a healthy discussion among program staff about their beliefs, values, and hopes for the program.

The second objective for the workshop participants is to identify the major information they need to collect to find out whether their assumptions are correct. The information from the workshop is used to design an evaluation plan that is responsive to the program's values and assumptions. This approach results in a conceptual model for the program that may or may not look like the traditional logic model. In fact, I never use the term *logic model* since it connotes an intellectualism that can come across as elitist, mysterious, and Western. This is not to argue that conceptualizing the program is not important. In fact, it is essential to good evaluation design. However, the model should fit the program and the stakeholders' way of seeing the program. Traditional logic modeling formats might be too sequential and narrative-driven and not appropriate ways to capture the connections between program activities and underlying assumptions in Indian Country.

Participatory Practice and Capacity Building. A third objective of the workshop is to establish a participatory ethic for the evaluation. Staff and other stakeholders should participate in developing their evaluation. In a setting that values community, participatory processes are recommended. Also, as a result of building a theory of change together, I become a partner in an evaluation process that is owned by the program staff and stakeholders. The partnership builds relationships between program operations and the evaluation—between the program staff and the evaluator. This approach fits in the emerging indigenous framework because it demonstrates that the evaluation is *respectful* of the vision of the program held by its primary stakeholders and establishes *relationship* in executing the evaluation—two of Christensen's three R's (2002).

Given the high value tribal communities place on sovereignty and self-determination, it is recommended that evaluators look for opportunities to build evaluation capacity whenever possible. Using a participatory workshop to build the program's conceptual model and evaluation plan demystifies the process of evaluation and builds ownership in the evaluation. Other opportunities for building capacity should be explored. Many tribes sponsor their own community colleges, and this may be a way to build evaluation training capacity for budding evaluators from Indian Country. In one of my projects, which involved a large community survey, I was able to work with college students who were interning with the tribal office during the summer. They assisted in recruiting focus group participants, developing questions for the survey, and administering the survey at community events and meetings. Although these opportunities might be rare, a responsive evaluator should be aware that they are possible and try to incorporate as much training as possible in the evaluation plan.

Issues in Using Qualitative and Quantitative Methods. Given the highly contextual nature of tribal programs (operating in their sense of place and community), qualitative methods are central to the work. This is not to say that quantitative inquiry is not valued; rather, tribal communities have simply not found it a useful way to assess merit. Tribal populations in the programs being evaluated are often not large enough to put faith in statistical models; as a result statistical analysis is usually limited to descriptive summaries. Experimental design is generally discouraged, for ethical and practical reasons. It is difficult to assign adults or children into different "treatment groups" in small communities. Even if this could be done, the social and political reaction to a perception of unequal treatment could be quite disruptive in a small and fragile community.

Confidentiality is an important concern in both qualitative and quantitative approaches. When working in small communities, evaluators have to continually sort out information that does not protect the confidentiality of the respondent. When we asked a group of evaluators with experience in Indian Country to identify challenges in doing evaluation in tribal communities, one evaluator noted that her dilemma concerned how disposition of data influences accessibility to participants. She found that fear of repercussions if identity were figured out from responses to ethnographic inquiry or survey answers can discourage participation or response rate (Greenman, e-mail communication, 2003).

Furthermore, instrumentation can be problematic, especially when the funders require standardized measures. Another evaluator responded to our request for challenges by noting that she was being required to use a one-hundred-page intake form that was proving impossible to administer. When she undertook a cultural core measures search, she found few culturally validated measures for American Indians (Kumpfer, e-mail communication, 2003) and none that she could use. Most previously developed instruments need to be reviewed and often revised to fit the context of an

Indian reservation or community. Survey questionnaires have to be developed to fit the general education level in the community, which is often lower than in mainstream communities. It is important to test items on a cross-section of the community, because advisory committees often have a higher level of education or literacy than the general population.

Trimble (1977) describes an effort to measure self-esteem of Indian adults. The Association of American Indian Social Workers, sponsors of the survey, formed an advisory board to guide development of the instrument. Their goal was to develop a standardized instrument that could be used by Indians who were members of various tribes. He noted that there were culturally based objections to creating one instrument that would work across the diversity of tribal nations. However, a core of the advisory committee did not want to abandon the idea of using one instrument. The compromise was an instrument that included open-ended and sentence-completion items to capture personal expression.

The ethics of evaluation require informed consent of those being interviewed. However, special care should be taken when interviewing across cultures. In my summary of conversation among Indian evaluators attending a conference sponsored by NSF, I share Christensen's concern that elders often think that everything they say will be reported, and they do not understand that in a final document only certain quotes often represent their interview. Christensen argues that informed consent is "making sure that the evaluators comprehend what you are saying, and that you understand and consent to how what you are saying will be used" (LaFrance, 2002a, p. 67).

Challenges in Doing Comparative Research. Varying tribal histories, locations, resources, and size make it difficult to draw conclusions across tribal communities. Case studies and qualitative approaches that embed the program within the context of the community are generally more effective than quantitative studies that seek comparison across communities or groups of tribal people. However, summative evaluation is often informed through comparison. So how do you find comparison groups? Obviously it depends on the service or program under consideration, but here are a few suggestions:

Using retrospective measures. This method allows participants to assess their own changes on the basis of personal perspectives. This approach is good when a premeasure instrument might be intrusive or intimidating to program participants.

Comparing tribal statistics with national data. Many national surveys contain data disaggregated by ethnicity. In some programs, the data on Indians contained in these data banks might be usefully compared to tribal data on the same measures.

Finding a comparison reservation community that is willing to act as a "control group." However, if this method is used, it is important to negotiate an understanding with the partner reservation so they are comfortable with the use of the evaluation findings.

General Advice to Evaluators. One of the guiding questions for this volume is, "How does better understanding of the role of culture improve evaluation practice?" Understanding the influence of tribal culture and context is critical when conducting evaluations in Indian communities. The goals of social services and educational programs are often twofold: help the individual student or client, and attempt to strengthen the community's health and well-being. Given this dual set of goals, indicators of success might not correspond to the dominant society's focus on individual achievement. These same values influence how tribal people view the role of researchers. Crazy Bull (1997) described these values in her advice to researchers who come into Indian Country: "We, as tribal people, want research and scholarship that preserves, maintains, and restores our traditions and cultural practices. We want to restore our homelands; revitalize our traditional religious practices; regain our health; and cultivate our economic, social, and governing systems. Our research can help us maintain our sovereignty and preserve our nationhood" (p. 17).

To ground the evaluation in the tribal community, a culturally responsive evaluator should learn as much as possible about its history, resources, governance, and composition. If possible, he or she should engage in community activities such as graduation ceremonies and dinners for the elders in the tribe, or funerals for honored tribal members. Engagement can also involve attending special events such as a Treaty Day celebration, powwow or tribal dance, rodeo or canoe journey. This participation can help the evaluator understand the context in which he or she is working. It also allows Indians in the community to build relationships with evaluators that are based on friendliness and respectful interest, rather than defined by strict roles and outsider "expertise." In fact, expertise in the form of education, degrees of higher learning, or professional reputation is of little value in Indian Country if the community does not see the evaluator as respectful and capable of understanding an indigenous perspective.

Building a strong partnership between the stakeholders and the evaluator and being willing to relinquish some of the power embedded in being "the evaluator" challenges long-held assumptions that an evaluator is to be impartial and distant from the program's operations. These assumptions are based on the need for objectivity in research and evaluation. However, partnership with the program being evaluated or with the community who are recipients of the program services does not imply that an evaluator loses the ability to remain objective. There is always some level of subjectivity influencing an evaluator's approach to her trade. This subjectivity is conditioned by the training and orientation (quantitative, qualitative, feminist, empiricist, critical, and so on) of the evaluator.

Evaluation methods that are responsive to community values and contexts are still objective in application if the evaluator and the program's stakeholders value learning from the evaluation. Situating evaluation methodology within an indigenous framework should result in creating this sense of ownership. Once ownership is created, the stakeholders value the knowledge they can gain from the evaluation—and evaluation is all about creating knowledge. When the stakeholders own knowledge creation, the evaluator can discuss negative findings (failure to accomplish goals, assumptions that appear to be incorrect) as well as positive findings. The knowledge becomes empowering, and evaluation is not viewed as merely a judgmental activity imposed by funding agencies or other outsiders.

By making the process of knowledge creation transparent and participatory, the evaluator builds evaluation capacity in tribal communities. It has been gratifying to be asked to review rough drafts of proposals in communities where I have conducted evaluations and see that they have included sophisticated evaluation designs using such terms as *theory of change, matrices of evaluation questions,* and *data collection plans.* It is also satisfying for an evaluator to become accepted and welcomed, not just for her trade but also as a friend and colleague in working toward the aspirations and sovereignty of the tribe. If the tools of the evaluator are used to fulfill the goals and aspirations of tribal peoples, then the evaluator has given back to the community, and not just come in to assess, monitor, and judge. She and the community have a sense of reciprocity—the final *R* in Christensen's model of elder epistemology.

References

Cajete, G. *Native Science: Natural Laws of Interdependence.* Santa Fe, N.M.: Clear Light, 2000.

Christensen, R. "Cultural Context and Evaluation: A Balance of Form and Function." In *Workshop Proceedings of the Cultural Context of Educational Evaluation: A Native American Perspective.* Arlington, Va.: National Science Foundation, Apr. 2002.

Crazy Bull, C. "A Native Conversation About Research and Scholarship." *Tribal College Journal,* 1997, *9,* 17–23.

Deloria, V. *God Is Red: A Native View of Religion.* Golden, Colo.: Fulcrum, 1994.

Deloria, V. "Ethnoscience and Indian Realities. In B. Deloria, K. Foehner, and S. Scinta (eds.), *Spirit and Reason: The Vine Deloria Reader.* Golden, Colo.: Fulcrum, 1999.

Garroutte, E. M. *Real Indians: Identity and the Survival of Native America.* Berkeley: University of California Press, 2003.

Govina, H. "Treaties and Traditions: Cultural Competencies in New Zealand Evaluation Design and Practice." Paper presented at the annual meeting of the American Evaluation Association, Washington, D.C., Nov. 2002.

Johnston, A. "Building Capacity: Ensuring Evaluation Findings Contribute to Program Growth." Paper presented at the annual meeting of the American Evaluation Association, Washington, D.C., 2002.

LaFrance, J. "Redefining American Indian Education: Evaluation Issues in Tribally Controlled Schools." Unpublished doctoral dissertation, Harvard University, 1990.

LaFrance, J. "Networking: How to Develop a Line of Communications." In *Workshop*

Proceedings of the Cultural Context of Educational Evaluation: A Native American Perspective. Arlington, Va.: National Science Foundation, 2002a.

LaFrance, J. "The Role of an External Evaluator at a Small Tribal College." Paper presented at the annual meeting of the American Evaluation Association, Washington, D.C., 2002b.

Smith, L. T. *Decolonizing Methodologies: Research and Indigenous Peoples.* London: Zed Books, 1999.

Swisher, K. G. "From Passive to Active: Research in Indian Country." *Tribal College Journal,* 1993, 4(3), 4–5.

Trimble, J. E. "The Sojourner in the American Indian Community: Methodological Issues and Concerns." *Journal of Social Issues,* 1977, 33(4), 159–174.

Weiss, C. H. *Evaluation.* (2nd ed.) Upper Saddle River, N.J.: Prentice Hall, 1998.

JOAN LAFRANCE is an independent evaluator and the owner of Mekinak Consulting based in Seattle, Washington, specializing in working with American Indian and Alaska Native tribes and organizations.

4

This chapter describes two projects and develops from them a set of five factors that facilitate multicultural validity. The chapter also includes a discussion of some limitations of these case examples and suggestions for further testing and refinement of multicultural validity in the more general context of validity within the evaluation field.

Developing and Implementing Culturally Competent Evaluation: A Discussion of Multicultural Validity in Two HIV Prevention Programs for Latinos

Ross F. Conner

The evaluation field in the United States has seen an increase in evaluations with and of diverse cultural populations, including racial or ethnic populations as well as those cultures and subcultures with special interests, concerns, or needs, such as the youth and gay and lesbian communities. These evaluations have occurred as the populations grow in number and become more assertive in developing social programs and policies suited to their communities. To meaningfully assess and engage these culturally sensitive programs, evaluators need to develop and implement evaluations sensitive to the cultural issues that characterize and are important to the populations, as well as to program participants and stakeholders. This chapter describes programs developed for two populations of Latinos, discusses the evaluations that were developed and implemented for these programs, and moves to a discussion of five factors that fostered a culturally sensitive evaluation.

One helpful way that that the issue of cultural sensitivity in evaluation has been conceptualized is in terms of multicultural validity (Kirkhart, 1995, 1997, 1998). Kirkhart defines multicultural validity as "the accuracy, correctness, genuineness, or authenticity of understandings (and ultimately, evaluative judgments) across dimensions of cultural difference" (Conner and Kirkhart, 2003, p. 1). This construct highlights the importance of

NEW DIRECTIONS FOR EVALUATION, no. 102, Summer 2004 © Wiley Periodicals, Inc.

attending to cultural differences and cultural issues, specifically in regard to evaluation—to be sure there is valid understanding of the operation and outcomes of the program, so that valid conclusions and judgments ultimately can be made.

This concern for valid judgments and conclusions is at the core of evaluation (Patton, 1997; Rossi, Lipsey, and Freeman, 2003) and has underlain the long-standing interest within the evaluation field in developing methods that produce valid, as well as reliable, information on which to base conclusions. Campbell began the formulation of validity types and, with Stanley, set out the initial distinction between internal and external validity (Campbell and Stanley, 1963). Internal validity focused on whether a difference occurred that was caused by a special treatment or program; external validity was concerned with the generalizability of the effect to other groups, over different times and settings. Cook and Campbell (1979) expanded this validity formulation, and recently Shadish, Cook, and Campbell (2002) refined it further. Shadish, Cook, and Campbell specify four types of validity: internal, external, construct, and statistical conclusion. Internal and external validity essentially match the definitions that Campbell and Stanley gave earlier. Construct validity relates to the "validity of inferences about the higher order constructs that represent sampling particulars"; statistical conclusion validity is defined as "the validity of inferences about the correlation (covariation) between treatment and outcome" (p. 38).

Multicultural validity fits within three of these four categories: internal, external, and construct validity. Cultural issues and differences can be important factors in understanding which variables did and did not cause differences in programs (internal validity), which effects generalize over other settings and times (external validity), and what effects mean for higher-order constructs and implications (construct validity). Multicultural validity therefore extends the issues evaluators need to be attentive to if they are to draw valid conclusions, set out well-grounded implications, and make accurate recommendations.

In attending to multicultural issues, the evaluator cannot rely on the methodological, statistical, or technical adjustments that can be used for other validity concerns. Instead, the evaluator must learn about and respond to the context of the evaluation and its culturally related components, as well as to the participants in the evaluation and the cultural issues relevant to them. For example, an evaluator who learns about and understands the importance of elders within a particular culture could work with a group of elders to enlist the cooperation and involvement of those members of the community from whom the evaluator wants valid information. Without the involvement of the elders, the community members might not participate at all, or if they do, they might give inaccurate information.

At this early stage in the development of an awareness of and approaches to multicultural validity, examples are the best learning resource. From these examples, we also can begin to develop a typology of issues that evaluators might attend to in increasing the multicultural validity of their work. This paper presents two examples of evaluations in culturally anchored contexts and concludes with an initial listing of factors for evaluators to consider in increasing the multicultural validity of their work. Both of the illustrative projects focused on HIV prevention among Latinos but with different populations of Latinos.

Case Studies

The two case studies that follow highlight issues related to multicultural diversity.

Case One: Tres Hombres sin Fronteras. The Tres Hombres sin Fronteras (Three Men Without Borders) program was developed by and for Latino farmworkers. The program focused on educating Latino male farmworkers about the threat of HIV/AIDS posed by unprotected sexual contact with sex workers. The educational message was mainly disseminated via a *fotonovela,* an eight-page picture comic book that tells the story of three farmworkers who cross the U.S.-Mexico border to work in the agricultural fields.

The story follows the three lead characters, Marco, Sergio, and Victor, as they are introduced to after-work temptations, such as the sex workers who are typically and regularly brought into migrant labor camps. The sex workers featured in the fotonovela include Karla, a "high-class" sex worker, and Lucy, a sex worker more typical of those brought into the camps. At the suggestion of the farmworkers involved in developing the program, Karla is the main AIDS educator in terms of explaining the need for and advocating the use of a condom. The men felt that a high-class sex worker like Karla, whose business is sexual contacts, would have credibility with farmworker readers to convey the HIV prevention message. Marco, the farmworker in the story who is the "good model" with whom the reader is to identify, receives and heeds Karla's message about the need to use a condom. As the story progresses, he does not contract AIDS and returns to Mexico to rejoin his wife and family. Lucy, the other sex worker featured in the fotonovela, does not advocate the use of condoms and pays the consequences in the story. She not only contracts AIDS but also passes it to her farmworker clients, in particular Sergio, the "bad model" of the three men featured in the story. Sergio passes HIV to his wife, and she passes the virus to their new baby.

Formative evaluation of the fotonovela indicated a need for a supplemental brochure, using the same picture-book approach, that showed how to use a condom and where to obtain one and had several sample condoms attached. With farmworkers as advisors, a supplemental booklet with this content was produced, pilot-tested, and included with the fotonovela ("Marco Aprende como Protegerse"—Marco Learns How to Protect Himself) The educational program therefore consisted of the fotonovela and the special supplemental mini-fotonovela.

This HIV prevention program used a nondidactic, visual approach appropriate to the men for whom it was intended. It also used a format, a fotonovela, with which they were familiar but that was at that time novel for U.S.-based AIDS education. Other components of the program and its development are described in Mishra and Conner (1996).

Case One: Evaluation Description. The evaluation, like the program, was developed with the involvement and significant input of migrant farmworkers, working through long-standing community health clinics that served these men. (I am grateful to many individuals at these clinics and on the study team for their assistance in developing and implementing the evaluation.) The goal was to test the effectiveness of the educational program in changing HIV-related knowledge, attitudes, and practices. To accomplish this goal, the effects of the fotonovela were tested in a quasi-experimental study that involved matched camps of farmworkers who received the program either initially or at a later point. Ten migrant camps located in the same geographical area but physically separated from each other were matched and paired for their approximate similarity on a small set of dimensions: size, composition, and housing conditions. One camp in each pair was randomly selected to receive the program initially (the "treatment" condition); the other camp, the "comparison" condition, received the program about a month later but until that time served as a control. Offering the program to everyone, some sooner and some later, accommodated both the wishes of the farmworkers who advised on the study and the needs of the evaluation design to detect causal links between the program and HIV-related changes.

Farmworkers in all camps were surveyed about HIV/AIDS-related knowledge, attitudes, and behaviors at two time points: before anyone received the program, and about a month later after the treatment group received the program. The surveys were developed with special care to their format and content. The farmworkers were generally low-literacy, Spanish-only speakers from rural areas in Mexico. Their average educational level was four years of total schooling, so their Spanish reading and writing abilities were limited. These factors meant that a written survey could not be used. In addition, individual interviews were not possible, owing to study resource constraints, and would not have been feasible in any case, given the working and living conditions of the farmworkers. Instead, we used a small-group, oral-and-written survey format. Men in each small group received a large set of questions and answers written in Spanish. Each question and its associated answers, in content and format, were duplicated on a flipchart sheet. A native Spanish-speaking facilitator read each question, following with his hand the words on the flipchart sheet as he spoke. This process allowed a farmworker who did not read Spanish to understand the questions and answers and to "icon match," rather than read, in selecting an answer. This process lengthened the sessions but it gave a friendly, human quality to the survey procedure that farmworkers enjoyed. Each man received five dollars in cash for his participation in an interview.

The content of the questions was also geared to and organized for the participants. Because personal, sexually focused questions are a sensitive topic among the population of farmworkers, it was important first to establish good rapport and trust among the participants and the facilitator. For this reason, the first questions focused on nonsensitive, easy-to-answer topics such as location of birth and marital status. This section included some discussion among the men of selected questions, to establish a relaxed atmosphere. Once rapport was built among the participants and the facilitator, the questions progressed to more sensitive reports on recent sexual actions with different types of individuals (for example, a sex worker). This procedure was developed from the suggestions of farmworkers who served as informal advisors during the development of the questions and procedures. The procedures were refined during pilot testing, in which participants were questioned about their reactions to the questions and their willingness to answer questions truthfully. We had a high level of confidence that men were willing and able to answer the questions accurately and honestly.

At the end of the study, 89 men were surveyed twice across the two study conditions. Although this was a decrease from the 150 men who were surveyed initially, the drop-off appeared to result from factors unrelated to the study conditions that were shared among camps (that is, a man might have been let go from a job, returned to Mexico for personal reasons, or was deported by immigration authorities). Comparability checks of men in the two study groups generally showed that the treatment and comparison groups were similar at the pretest.

Posttest results, in sum, showed positive effects from the program. In brief, posttest comparisons indicated significant but small changes in HIV/AIDS-related knowledge, significant changes in HIV/AIDS-related attitudes related to the program content, and increases in the target behavior (reported condom use with a sex worker) in the treatment group, but not in the comparison group. More details about and caveats associated with these results are presented in Mishra and Conner (1996).

Case Two: Proyecto SOLAAR. The SOLAAR program ("Superacion, Orgullo y Lucha Atraves de Amor en Relaciones; un programa de prevencion y educacion del VIH para hombres latinos"—empowerment, pride, and struggle through love in relationships: an HIV prevention and education program for Latino men) focused on Spanish-speaking gay and bisexual Latino men in a large urban setting. Proyecto SOLAAR was developed by men from this population who noted the special needs of this subgroup of urban Latino men and their unique HIV risk factors. These men are caught between two cultures: the Latino culture from which they came and the Anglo culture, particularly the urban Anglo-dominated gay culture, into which they immigrated. These two cultures differ in their assumptions about particular issues related to relationships between people. The resulting misunderstandings from these differences can put these Latino men at risk for HIV/AIDS. The SOLAAR program was developed to help men recognize these issues and to take actions to deal with them that would reduce their risks of HIV/AIDS. (See Conner and others, forthcoming, for a fuller description of the SOLAAR program and its evaluation.)

One example of these issues is the topic of dating. In U.S. culture, dating is a way for people to get to know each other before making any serious commitments for a longer-term relationship. In Mexico, the country from which the majority of men come, the same concept of "dating" does not exist. Instead, a couple (generally a heterosexual couple) undertaking this same sort of dating behavior is understood to be well along on a path leading to a long-term relationship, in particular, marriage. When a gay or bisexual man from Mexico begins and continues a dating relationship with an Anglo-culture man in the United States, he often assumes, frequently unconsciously, that the commitment to a long-term relationship is greater than what his Anglo-culture partner assumes, also frequently unconsciously. This unrecognized but operational cultural misunderstanding can lead the Latino man to engage in riskier sexual behaviors (such as unprotected sex) than are warranted during dating in a U.S. context. In addition, the men's differing expectations about what dating implies can undermine the development of a long-term relationship, resulting in frustration and challenges to self-esteem. Proyecto SOLAAR was developed to surface issues such as relationship, communication, and self-esteem in a nonthreatening way, and then to assist men in developing effective ways to engage in positive, healthy relationships. By addressing these issues, the program aims to reduce HIV risk behaviors.

The core of the program is a day-long "retreat," conducted mostly in Spanish, during which a small group of men discuss issues and engage in some exercises and games that focus on topics that include relationships, dating, communication, self-concept, and HIV/AIDS. Held at a hotel and including several meals and small gifts, the session is facilitated by two SOLAAR staff members, who set an informal, conversational tone and foster an open, frank exchange. By the end of the day, the participants have developed a "dating plan" and "HIV risk reduction plan" that they are encouraged to put into action. The plan differs for each participant according to his current behavior, needs, interests, and desired outcomes. About a month after the retreat, a half-day reunion is held and the participants come together to share their experiences in implementing their plans and to revise their plans.

Case Two: Evaluation Description. The evaluation for the program was developed with input from SOLAAR program staff, who work closely with prospective program participants. The evaluation was then refined and revised with staff and participant input. (I thank the staff of Proyecto SOLAAR and the members of the evaluation team for their assistance in developing and implementing the evaluation.) The general approach involves comparing men who participated in the program with men who did not. These men were followed over time with pretest and several posttest measures. The evaluation is currently in progress, and data are being collected from the final sets of program participants using the pretest and posttest measures.

The evaluation measures were developed at the beginning of the program and were intensively pilot-tested and revised with program participants. These measures are individual, confidential surveys of demographic information (country of birth, income, relationship status, and so on), self-esteem and self-efficacy, communication skills, relationship behaviors, retreat-specific information and exercises (such as dating plans), and HIV risk behaviors as well as HIV/AIDS knowledge and attitudes. The surveys were originally developed in English and Spanish, but during pilot testing it became clear that Spanish-language versions were preferred by the men, even if they were fully bilingual. The surveys, which take about twenty to thirty minutes to complete, are used as a pretest measure prior to the retreat session and at several time points following the retreat as posttest measures. The pretest and first posttest measures are administered in person to men before and after the retreats and reunions; the second posttest is administered over the telephone about six months after the retreat. Men receive a twenty-five-dollar cash payment for each survey they complete.

Although the content and format of the measures have remained fairly constant, the evaluation plan in which they are used has evolved as program implementation progresses. The original evaluation plan was a quasi-experimental design involving two randomly composed groups: a treatment group and a delayed-treatment comparison group. Men who were interested in participating in the program were randomly assigned to one of two retreats, which were to be held a month apart. Men in both groups were to be given pretests at the same time point prior to the start of the first retreat and then tested again at several posttest points, as appropriate for each group. The delayed-treatment comparison group was to serve as a way to identify short-term changes (that is, after about one month) that were due to the program, after which this group became a treatment group when the second retreat was held.

During the initial months of the program implementation, it became apparent that this design and survey administration plan would not work. The number of men signing up for the program was too small to form two separate retreat groups, and it was not possible for men to arrange to take the pretest individually prior to the start of the retreat. Administering the pretest at the beginning of the retreat session, when the men first appeared, solved the latter problem. The former challenge resulted in a yearlong search for and creation of a recruitment campaign. This new program component, a special social marketing campaign, was developed collaboratively with the program and evaluation team members working together and with program participants themselves (both past and potential attendees). These men offered the most critical input on what would attract the attention and interest of prospective participants. In particular, the social marketing campaign used two humorous sketches of Latino gay or bisexual men to attract attention, along with a toll-free number and an Internet address for more information and initial contact with the program. More details of the campaign are described in Conner and others (2004).

The campaign was implemented and, over time, resulted in a significant increase in interest in the program. A new challenge arose, however, that necessitated additional adjustments in the evaluation design. Although more men were assigned to attend retreats, the number who actually showed up on the day of the retreat was low. Feedback from some of the no-show men indicated that their lack of participation is not related to a lack of interest in the program but instead to changes in work schedules and unexpected personal developments that men could not be aware of when they were assigned a retreat date (typically one to two months prior).

The current evaluation plan accommodates the men's situations, as we now better understand them. In terms of culturally related aspects, this revised plan recognizes and avoids the men's general reluctance to say no to someone offering a benefit. The current plan, with a choice of dates, allows men to choose a session that is genuinely better for them rather than being assigned to a session, which might or might not in fact be convenient. In addition, the revised plan accepts and capitalizes on other realities that cannot be changed, such as unexpected, late-breaking developments that prevent some men from attending. Retreats are still offered in pairs, but only one week apart, and men can attend either; they are assigned a date anywhere from a week to a month prior.

For the evaluation, a quasi-experimental comparison design is still being used, with two groups: men who attend a retreat and men who are scheduled to attend but do not show up. The no-show men are contacted by telephone soon after the scheduled retreat and administered the pretest survey. This current design has both advantages and disadvantages over the previous delayed-treatment comparison group design. One advantage is that men in the no-show comparison group do not receive the program and therefore become useful short- and long-term comparisons. One disadvantage is that men self-select into the program or no-show groups. Although informal information indicates that the reasons for showing or not showing up are unrelated to the program or its critical variables (self-efficacy, relationship skills), comparisons of pretest information between the program and no-program groups will help to confirm this.

As I have noted, the evaluation is in its final phase of data collection. The changes in the evaluation design will result in a mix of types and sizes of treatment and comparison groups. All evaluation study participants in all groups will have been surveyed at pretest; a smaller number will have been surveyed at the first posttest time (about a month after the retreat) and a smaller number yet at the second posttest (about six months after). The most complete data from the largest number of men will come from longitudinal comparisons of program participants. Data on short- and long-term nonparticipants will be more limited and used more for insights about the program's main effects than as a basis for definitive causal conclusions about them.

Factors That Increase Multicultural Validity

The two evaluations share five factors that helped to increase their validity, more specifically their multicultural validity. Together, these five factors constitute an initial typology that are proposed to increase multicultural validity. Three of them focus on issues that relate to evaluation planning, and two others relate to an approach to action during evaluation implementation.

Involving Participants in the Evaluation Study Planning. In both cases, the people who were centrally involved in the program were also important participants in the evaluation planning and pilot testing. The farmworkers in the Tres Hombres study and the Latino gay or bisexual men in the SOLAAR study provided suggestions about evaluation procedures and measurement content. This input occurred especially at the initial stages of evaluation planning and continued as needed throughout the implementation of the evaluation. In the SOLAAR case, for example, the participants offered information that was critical in developing the new social marketing plan devised to increase program recruitment. Participants' comments also afforded valuable insights into how to revise the evaluation design to accommodate the participants while maintaining the quasi-experimental approach. Specifically, Latino men's reluctance to say no was clear during the focus group sessions; men would not speak against any of the many social marketing campaign themes presented to them, even though there were no consequences for positive or negative judgments. Observing this characteristic during the focus group sessions from behind a one-way mirror, the research team learned that any aspects of the evaluation design or measures that inadvertently fostered yes responses or confronted men with take-it-or-leave-it options should be changed. As explained earlier, the new evaluation design gives men an option of sessions to attend rather than only one take-it-or-leave-it choice.

The uniqueness of these evaluation contexts raises an issue: Can culturally sensitive evaluation perhaps only be possible in conjunction with a program that is also culturally sensitive? In the Tres Hombres and SOLAAR programs, the program development and service staff members had long histories of working with their special populations and in some instances were from these populations themselves. These staff members therefore not only spoke the language (literally) of their clients but also lived the experience. Although this type of staffing does not guarantee culturally sensitive staff, it increases the likelihood of having an appropriate staff. In addition, in developing and implementing the program activities, the staff members incorporated their understanding of the cultures of the men. For example, in the SOLAAR program, the retreat day started not at 8:00 A.M. but instead shortly before noon and began with a good, full meal. Doing evaluation within a program context that is already culturally sensitive brings a significant advantage in fostering multicultural validity.

Speaking the Literal Language of the Participants. An obvious first step in ensuring multicultural validity is using the same language as the participants. In the case of the Tres Hombres and SOLAAR projects, Spanish was clearly the main language of the programs' clients and therefore needed to be the language of the program's services and its evaluation.

Although speaking in the language of the participants would seem to be an easy task for the evaluator to implement, there can be degrees of language use to attend to, both in speaking and in writing. In the SOLAAR program, for example, the men generally spoke Spanish. In some cases, however, men spoke a melange of Spanish and English (what some men called "Spanglish") or in a few rare cases mostly English. Fortunately, the men themselves are used to these variations in Spanish-English usage and tend to accommodate them spontaneously themselves by, for example, offering intermittent translation to a mostly English-speaking participant. The evaluation team member who administered the surveys and therefore had direct contact with the men was always someone who spoke and wrote good or excellent Spanish and excellent English and was at ease with Spanglish as well. Consequently he was able to explain survey items or answer questions in the language that fit the participant.

Although the correct level of spoken language was important in the Tres Hombres program evaluation, the correct level of the written language was a bigger concern. Preliminary work on the evaluation made it clear that most of the farmworkers had very limited reading ability in Spanish but were also reluctant to admit this limitation to others, whether members of the program, evaluation team, or fellow farmworkers. The evaluation surveys were designed with these realities in mind. A self-administered written survey was not used; an oral survey was used instead, with written question-and-answer options, supplemented by a large-scale visual representation of each set of answer options. This process allowed men who did not read Spanish well to follow the written questions and response options by listening to the evaluation staff member. Participants were then able to match what was said to what was on the sheet in front of them. All information on the paper was duplicated exactly on the flipchart sheet for use as a visual guide. If necessary, then, men could icon-match instead of read, keeping their literacy level private and answering the questions accurately. Even men able to read sometimes found the icon-matching approach easier when coupled with the oral presentation of all question-and-answer options (for example, thinking such as "the second option that he read and that's on his chart is the one I'm picking for my answer"). In terms of fostering multicultural validity, a significant benefit of this written-oral-icon approach is that, once refined and pilot-tested, respondents can quickly and almost unconsciously understand and use it. Many of us unconsciously match icons already. For those who are uneasy about their literacy level, the approach is a way to step around literacy problems that does not intimidate or denigrate but instead affirms and assists. In a small way, this process can also improve reading ability, if, as in Tres Hombres, many of the answer options were repeated orally and visually many times.

Speaking the Figurative Language of the Participants. Evaluators need to speak not only the literal language of the participants but also the figurative language. Figurative language relates to the content and style of communication, both oral and written. The content and style must match that of the participants if multicultural validity is to be achieved in evaluation.

The contrast between some of the survey answer options for the men in SOLAAR and the farmworkers in Tres Hombres illustrates this point. Some of the SOLAAR survey question options were grids, with questions down the first column and Likert-type response options across the top row. Men were to select the appropriate box for each question. This complex grid approach was not appropriate for the men in Tres Hombres. Each question needed its own set of answers, with one question given at a time. Repetition was not a problem for the farmworkers and in fact was an asset; it reaffirmed their understanding of response options. For the men in SOLAAR, on the other hand, repeating questions with a set of similar response options would have quickly bored them and possibly undermined the accuracy of their answers. The grid was much more efficient and had the additional benefit of allowing a man to consider several questions at once, particularly vis-à-vis his answers to each.

Working Collaboratively with Participants During Implementation. An evaluator can think about and attend to the previous factors during the planning phase of the evaluation. This factor, working collaboratively, and the related final one, sharing the benefits, relate more to the implementation phase of the evaluation and are of a different type than the previous three factors. This factor and the next one focus on an ongoing approach to action, rather than on particular issues.

Evaluation activities largely occur in uncontrollable settings in the field—in communities, in schools, in homes, in the offices of organizations and businesses—where many unexpected factors can arise that impinge on the conduct of evaluation. Consequently, the evaluator has to be ready to recognize and accommodate these factors in the evaluation work. Culturally based evaluations are no different and can be subject to a greater-than-average number of uncertainties, depending on the nature of the program and the participants. Working collaboratively with program staff and participants is one effective approach in maintaining the validity of the evaluation. This approach is similar to those used in and advocated for effective community-based evaluation, much of which involves culturally based and multicultural issues (Conner and others, 2004).

The Tres Hombres and SOLAAR evaluations were conducted using a collaborative approach with the staff and program participants. The evaluators recognized that they did not have all the knowledge necessary to plan and implement a good, valid evaluation; the knowledge of the staff and participants was critical to the effort. As the evaluations were implemented, a good, collegial, working relationship was essential to learn about and deal with unexpected challenges and new developments. Additionally, a collaborative relationship increases the possibility that new opportunities will be recognized and therefore increases the number of changes that can be incorporated into and benefit the evaluation. These points are exemplified next.

In the case of Tres Hombres, the participants' ideas about ways to guarantee attendance at the posttest sessions were very beneficial. Participants suggested that special blue cards be given to each farmworker after the pretest, on which his posttest date and time were listed. This simple task turned out to be an effective tool; the blue cards were prized by the farmworkers (for whom they certified a man's participation in an important project) and were usually proudly presented at the posttest (although this was not a condition for participation).

The need for increased recruitment into the SOLAAR program was completely unanticipated at the outset of that evaluation but became clear when limited numbers caused the implementation of the evaluation design to be suspended. The collaborative relationship among the service and evaluation teams as well as with some past participants was the basis on which to identify the challenge in a productive, "we're in this together" way, avoiding blaming and finger pointing, and moving forward productively and creatively in developing a solution. The service and evaluation teams stepped aside and followed others' guidance, in this case the social marketing consultant and past participants, with benefits for the program and its evaluation.

Working collaboratively over the long run involves a different type of relationship between the evaluator and the program than what is typically described where the evaluator takes a hands-off, detached stance in relation to the program. As the Proyecto SOLAAR examples in this chapter illustrate, the evaluators positioned themselves in that evaluation as support to the program, midway between being critics or advocates of it.

Sharing the Benefits. The final factor is a special subset of the previous factor, working collaboratively. As part of collaboration, the benefits of working together must be shared among the partners, not only so that there is some equity in resource distribution but also so that recognition, thanks, and appreciation are shared among the partners in ways that accommodate all the partners. Sharing benefits in various ways further strengthens the partnership so that it can continue to confront and overcome challenges in order that both the program and its evaluation proceed.

In the Tres Hombres program, benefits were shared in different ways. Farmworkers were paid a small (but for them at the time significant) amount for each survey they completed. They also received other benefits from participation in the evaluation, apart from those directly associated with the content of the program, one of which was, for many men, a sense of personal importance from participating in a study to improve the health of migrant farmworkers. This feeling of importance was powerfully demonstrated during the formation phase of the evaluation, when a group of farmworkers met to comment on the program focus (HIV risks) and materials and on the evaluation instruments. The men had so much to contribute that the session lasted much longer than anticipated. Finally, the facilitator ended the meeting, gave them their cash payment, and thanked them for their comments and suggestions. The men also wanted to thank the facilitator for meeting with them. Spontaneously, the men went into the fields, picked what was ripe at that time, and stuffed the cab and trunk of the facilitator's car with lettuce heads as their way of sharing and returning benefits. This gesture made the rest of the evaluation team even more committed to conducting a good evaluation.

Similar sharing of benefits has occurred in the SOLAAR program. The men were paid for each evaluation survey session at a rate (twenty-five dollars) that offers meaningful and tangible benefits. This payment not only recognizes the importance of their time but also fosters a conscientious and thoughtful approach to answering the evaluation survey questions, which has clear benefits for increased validity. The payment also increases the likelihood that men will participate in the six-month follow-up posttest. Although they are happy to have these cash benefits, some of the men have also expressed their willingness to participate in surveys from their desire to give back and contribute to a program they have enjoyed and see as beneficial.

Another important level of sharing of benefits occurred for the SOLAAR program, between the program and evaluation teams. In addition to periodic meals together serving as minicelebrations to recognize and nurture the partnership, the team members participate together in professional meetings and sessions to share information about the program in paper or poster formats and to increase their general skills and knowledge. Funds in the evaluation budget pay for expenses to attend these professional meetings. Sharing of benefits in these ways has nurtured the partnership and increased the degree of cooperation among the team members, as they adapt to new program realities and challenges. Because of this partnership and cooperation, each team member better understands the needs of the other team members and is more willing to find solutions to problems that benefit everyone if possible. For example, throughout the changes in the evaluation plan, a quasi-experimental comparison component of one type or another has been maintained. In addition, sufficient time and a quiet environment are always set aside at the beginning and end of each retreat and each reunion for evaluation surveys. This ensures that the data are of high quality and not subject to problems of incompleteness and inaccuracy that typically occur in the chaotic, rushed conditions when evaluation forms are distributed as participants leave a session.

Conclusion

This chapter has described two cases where evaluations were conducted in ways that recognized and built upon culturally based aspects of the programs. Five factors were identified in both evaluations that helped to foster multicultural validity. In closing this paper, several aspects of this discussion need to be highlighted.

First, it should be noted that these two evaluations were not undertaken with the conscious intent of maximizing multicultural validity but instead with the more general intent of maximizing validity, in the spirit of Campbell (1963) and more recently of Shadish and Cook (2002). The multicultural framework has been placed around the evaluations after the fact. The five described factors were also identified after the fact, or more accurately in the case of the SOLAAR program during the fact because that study is still under way. It would be beneficial for the advancement of evaluation practice to put some of these factors to a proactive test, where these factors are consciously applied for their hypothesized effect on multicultural validity. It is necessary to create measures of the presence and extent of each factor and use these measures before, during, and after the evaluation. In addition, a measure of multicultural validity is needed to make comparisons between evaluations about the degree to which they achieve multicultural validity. In this chapter, the evidence for the multicultural validity of the evaluations presented is anecdotal and its objectivity is suspect, because of the lack of an independent author or evaluator. Independent observers should do future studies of multicultural validity, perhaps as part of meta-evaluations.

Second, the two cases presented here were selected because they both focus on a similar, general culturally based group (Latino males) and focus on a similar program theme (HIV prevention). These cases were not selected because they are necessarily the best cases of evaluation in terms of multicultural validity. Rather, they are proposed as good cases. At this early stage in the development of a typology of and conceptual framework for multicultural validity, it would be instructive to look retrospectively at culturally based cases where multicultural validity was judged to be low. What factors operated to restrict validity? Were any of the five factors identified here also operating, but perhaps in another way, in these unsuccessful cases? Cases thought to have positive outcomes in terms of high multicultural validity, such as those presented here, as well as cases that had negative outcomes can yield instructive leads to advance our thinking.

Finally, discussions of multicultural validity need to be anchored within the more general discussions in the evaluation field of validity, using Shadish, Cook, and Campbell's four-component framework (2002). By using this framework, we can make contributions to the larger discussions of evaluation design and contribute to the incremental growth in knowledge about how to do better field experiments and evaluations (Shadish, Cook, and Campbell, 2002).

Another advantage is that consideration of multicultural validity will be integrated more fully into evaluation practice of all types and not restricted to evaluation studies on programs that are, on the surface, culturally based. The five factors described here could be beneficial in evaluations of all types and all focuses. Attention to multicultural validity could be a catalyst for evaluation to revisit some of its old assumptions and practices, as well as establish new approaches and methods to furnish better data that reflect the realities of evaluations for many stakeholders.

References

Campbell, D. T., and Stanley, J. C. *Experimental and Quasi-Experimental Designs for Research.* Skokie, Ill.: Rand McNally, 1963.

Conner, R. F. *Principles of Community-Based Evaluation.* Irvine: Center for Community Health Research, University of California Irvine, 2004.

Conner, R. F., and Kirkhart, K. E. "Boundaries, Borderlands and Border-Crossers: Notes from a Dialog on Theory and Practice." Document developed for workshop, Hazel Symonette (organizer and chair), American Evaluation Association Annual Convention, Reno, Nev., Nov. 5–9, 2003.

Conner, R. F., and others. "Capacity-Building in an HIV Prevention Program for Gay and Bisexual Latino Men: Developing a Social Marketing Campaign to Assist Service Provision and Evaluation." In R. Myrick, B. Aoki, and S. Truax (eds.), *Using Community Collaborative Research to Build HIV Prevention Capacity: Results from the California Collaborative Research Initiative (AIDS Education and Prevention),* 2004.

Cook, T. D., and Campbell, D. T. *Quasi-Experimentation: Design and Analysis Issues for Field Settings.* Skokie, Ill.: Rand McNally, 1979.

Kirkhart, K. E. "Seeking Multicultural Validity: A Postcard from the Road." *Evaluation Practice,* 1995, *16*(1), 1–12.

Kirkhart, K. E. "Racism and Issues of Multicultural Validity in Evaluation Theory." Paper presented at the 105th Annual Convention of the American Psychological Association, Chicago, Aug. 1997.

Kirkhart, K. E. "Multicultural Validity and Social Justice." Paper presented at Evaluation '98, annual meeting of the American Evaluation Association, Chicago, Nov. 1998.

Mishra, S. I., and Conner, R. F. "Evaluation of an HIV Prevention Program Among Latino Farmworkers." In S. I. Mishra, R. F. Conner, and J. R. Magana (eds.), *AIDS Crossing Borders: The Spread of HIV Among Migrant Latinos.* Boulder, Colo.: Westview Press, 1996.

Patton, M. Q. *Utilization-Focused Evaluation.* Thousand Oaks, Calif.: Sage, 1997.

Rossi, P. H., Lipsey, M. W., and Freeman, H. E. *Evaluation: A Systematic Approach.* Thousand Oaks, Calif.: Sage, 2003.

Shadish, W. R., Cook, T. D., and Campbell, D. T. *Experimental and Quasi-Experimental Designs for Generalized Causal Inference.* Boston: Houghton Mifflin, 2002.

Ross F. Conner is director of the Center for Community Health Research at the University of California Irvine, where he is also on the faculty in the Planning, Policy and Design Department of the School of Social Ecology.

5

Bringing together individuals from cultural backgrounds with varied values and norms for expressing conflicting ideals can elevate the tensions inherent in participatory evaluation. As the authors of this chapter found out, even the most deliberate attention to cultural issues does not guarantee a smooth ride.

Lessons for Culturally Competent Evaluation from the Study of a Multicultural Initiative

Jean A. King, Julie E. Nielsen, Jeanette Colby

Here are the lessons that a team of evaluators learned during a study of a multicultural initiative in a large, Midwestern school district. During the evaluation process, three incidents brought the evaluators' multicultural best intentions into sharp focus. This chapter describes the evaluation's framework and process and then recasts the critical incidents as dilemmas, analyzing them to highlight the inherent challenges of culturally competent evaluation. We end with the implications of our experience for evaluation practice and theory.

The study began at the urging of the school district's coordinator of multicultural education and evolved for two years before it was finally funded. During that time, the coordinator—the idea champion for both multicultural education in the district and the study—got a new boss. A new superintendent had arrived and, in reorganizing the central office, appointed someone to lead Teaching and Instructional Services (TIS). With that person's approval, the study's planning moved forward. In large part he funded the evaluation in hopes of demonstrating in the gold standard of student achievement the value of millions of district dollars spent on a multicultural initiative over several years. The initiative included distinct programs at four sites: an elementary school whose entire focus was multicultural, a middle school "Afrocentric program," a high school infusing multiculturalism across its curriculum, and an innovative year-round school that sought to address the individual needs of a diverse student population.

NEW DIRECTIONS FOR EVALUATION, no. 102, Summer 2004 © Wiley Periodicals, Inc.

The evaluation team was aware of two broad concepts that necessarily framed the study: multicultural education, of which this initiative was an example, and cultural competence, which we sought to enact through our work. We knew these were complex constructs with multiple definitions and practical challenges. Scholars see multicultural education as a means for furthering the democratic aims of the United States, for promoting equity and social justice, and for preparing our youth to develop positive cross-cultural relationships that will be of benefit to our society (Banks, 1994; Bennett, 1986; Gay, 1987; Grant and Sleeter, 1986). Banks (1994) writes that true multicultural education requires comprehensive reform of the total school environment, yet in practice multicultural education is typically approached through incremental adjustments to existing settings.

Cultural competence is an equally challenging idea. The term *culture* refers to cognitive, affective, and behavioral patterns that human groups share, that is, the rules and norms by which people live; but there is little agreement on terminology (cultural competence, cultural sensitivity, cultural awareness), definitions, or core approaches. Both a process and a goal, cultural competence arises through a deliberate and continuous process of self and organizational introspection (Cross, Barzon, Dennis, and Isaacs, 1989; Lavizzo-Mourey and Mackenzie, 1996). To date, few scholars have conducted research on the extent to which cultural competence actually improves practice across multiple domains (education, health, mental health). In fact, Dean (2001) suggests that cultural competence as a construct is a myth and proposes instead . . . a model in which maintaining an awareness of one's lack of competence is the goal rather than the establishment of competence. With 'lack of competence' as the focus, a different view of practicing across cultures emerges. The client is the 'expert' and the clinician is in the position of seeking knowledge and trying to understand what life is like for the client. There is no thought of competence—instead one thinks of gaining understanding (always partial) of a phenomenon that is evolving and changing" (p. 624).

Laird (1998) encourages people to engage in an ongoing process of understanding about others. In this view, one operates from a position of "not-knowing" but should be an "informed non-knower" (p. 23).

Given the lack of directive clarity in the multicultural education literature and the literature on cultural competence, the evaluation literature—particularly that on participatory approaches—ultimately provided the conceptual framework for the study. A participatory approach, including significant involvement in the evaluation by those who were part of the programs studied, offered a viable means to address the complexity of the multicultural initiative. Participatory evaluations recognize multiple perspectives of knowledge and assume that participants in the evaluation process create shared meaning. In participatory approaches, evaluators seek firsthand experience with program activities and settings and, by facilitating the development of better informed program staff and participants, serve an essential function for improvement (Cousins and Whitmore, 1998; King, 1998; Weaver and Cousins, 2001).

By capturing the values and needs the evaluation participants represent, the evaluator serves as a facilitator of the program portrayal. Instead of imposing an external set of values and criteria, a participatory approach seeks to include and legitimize the perspectives of all individuals and groups in the program being evaluated. In some cases—as was largely true in the study described here—the determination of the program's merit or worth is not even in question. Multiple methods of inquiry ensure that the evaluation addresses the knowledge needs of multiple stakeholders and participants. Implicit in a participatory approach to program evaluation is a theory of use, supported by empirical evidence (Patton, 1997; Cousins, 2003), recognizing that multiple levels of use exist and that participants are often in the best position to determine how and when people will use evaluation findings.

The evaluation team understood that the setting for this study was complex, representing varied approaches to multicultural education as well as varied worldviews. It was always our assumption that, given these complexities, the questions this evaluation raised should be addressed through a participatory approach. Furthermore, we adopted the stance of informed not-knowers, fully anticipating that our evaluation participants would guide our understanding of the initiative according to the four sites' unique cultural milieus.

As originally proposed, the evaluation had four purposes. The first and second purposes were related: to document the implementation of district-supported multicultural activities at the four sites and then to determine lessons learned as a result. The third purpose—the key for the district office—was to explore the relationship between the multicultural initiative and achievement at these sites, first by developing a formal theory of action connecting multicultural activities with student learning, and second by studying the viability of using existing district achievement measures to evaluate the success of multicultural efforts. The study's final purpose was to develop a school-based model for assessing the implementation and effectiveness of multicultural programs, ensuring that staff could replicate the evaluation process developed. The study addressed these evaluation questions: (1) To what extent and in what ways has the multicultural initiative affected students' lives? (2) How do teachers and students from different cultural backgrounds build relations where the teacher teaches and the student learns in an environment that fosters a multicultural learning community where everyone teaches and learns? and (3) What do principals need to do to create a climate where people can discuss multicultural issues openly?

Applying the study's participatory framework, we made the design of the evaluation inclusive, applying multicultural thinking in four ways:

1. The members of the evaluation team, who represented four distinct cultural groups (including two evaluators of color), were committed to multicultural work, had a high level of cultural self-awareness, and clearly understood that cultural differences might affect the study.

2. With the support of the evaluation team, a multicultural steering committee (MSC), including culturally diverse members from the central office and liaisons from each site, ran the study. The group met monthly to make evaluation design and implementation decisions, including framing the evaluation questions, checking the instruments, analyzing the data, and ultimately developing recommendations. In addition, the MSC liaisons from each building coordinated communication and data collection for their sites, debriefing each month in the larger committee.

3. The evaluation process paid specific attention to relationship building in an interdependent social setting. In an effort to ensure that all voices were heard and that everyone could participate and be treated with respect, the group developed explicit ground rules for meetings that were later used to facilitate difficult discussions.

4. The MSC sponsored two evening meetings to purposefully reach out to the larger community in an effort both to authenticate program activities and materials and to ensure that the evaluation process and its outcomes were meaningful in a context broader than that of the district.

The MSC ultimately framed three questions for the study, and the team used a variety of data collection methods to answer them: document analysis, student focus groups, group interviews with parents, individual interviews with principals or designated site liaisons and four teachers at each site, observation in these teachers' classrooms, and staff surveys (King, Colby, Jeter, and Nielsen, 1999).

Was the study more successful—that is, better able to address our client's and stakeholders' concerns and answer their questions—because of our attention to multicultural issues? We would answer a guarded yes and give five reasons to support the claim. First, we succeeded in collecting data about a sensitive topic rarely discussed openly in the district, which is a large, highly centralized bureaucracy. Before we began, many told us it could not be done. To have succeeded at all was, in retrospect, no small accomplishment. Second, because of the multiple cultures present both on the evaluation team and on the MSC, differing cultural views informed the entire evaluation process from beginning to end. Representatives of African American, American Indian, and mainstream cultures regularly discussed the evaluation process, developed questions, reviewed surveys, and so on, ensuring interaction around potential problems throughout the study and reviewing the outcomes with an eye to differing cultural interpretations. (We did not, however, have participation from the Asian American or recent immigrant communities.) Third, as part of these conversations, the group raised and addressed difficult content—the dilemmas that will be discussed later—suggesting at least the face validity of the interactions. Fourth, although community involvement was undeniably limited, the group did make an effort and was partly successful in creating broader participation in the discussion. Finally, a few of the relationships begun as part of the study have continued since the evaluation ended, pointing to the viability of these interactions.

The Evaluators' Dilemmas That Emerged

Despite this evidence that the multicultural efforts were beneficial, there is also evidence suggesting the limitations of the process. At the start, the evaluation team was aware that there were four initiatives to be studied but knew little beyond that. As a first step in the study, team members wrote detailed descriptions of the multicultural activities at the sites to understand the variety of activities funded as part of the district initiative. We found that the programs differed on two key variables: cultural approach (culture-specific versus multicultural) and programmatic approach (targeted versus diffuse). Only one site used a culture-specific approach, that is, the curriculum and instruction offered an explicitly African American emphasis. The remaining three programs were multicultural in nature, infusing a variety of cultures in their curriculum and instruction. What quickly became clear was that the four programs bundled together under the label of a "multicultural initiative" applied dramatically different processes. Moreover, these differences contributed to a series of critical incidents that we have recast as "dilemmas" the evaluation team faced.

The first dilemma, an evaluation framing issue, raises the question, "How do you conduct a participatory evaluation when the cultures involved in the study have different expectations for teaching and learning?" On the one hand, each culture is unique and has a culturally valid, yet potentially different view of education. On the other hand, although we allow for cultural uniqueness, there remains a need to recognize social interdependence and the value of a common approach to public education.

A second dilemma poses a question regarding the proper role of evaluation in supporting the implementation of multicultural education. To bring social justice issues to the fore on the one hand, evaluations should yield accountability evidence, including instances of individuals who are "not with the program." On the other hand, however, there will always be a continuum in the implementation of a program, and evaluations should furnish evidence that supports meaningful change efforts and does not attack individuals. Shaming or blaming individuals is unlikely to lead to meaningful change.

Finally, the third dilemma, an issue of evaluation use, raises the question, "How can an evaluation frame meaningful study of a multicultural initiative that tackles an enduring social problem, especially one that may generate a politically correct set of responses?" On the one hand, it may seem impossible to effect change as the social context overwhelms every effort to do so, especially since people have a tendency to offer socially acceptable answers when asked to discuss sensitive issues. On the other hand, in every case evaluation has the potential to produce real information that, used well, can lead to meaningful and lasting reform.

A more detailed explication of each dilemma follows.

Dilemma One: "Teachers Teach and Students Learn, Right?" The first dilemma raises fundamental questions about teaching philosophies and the role of the teacher in a multicultural setting. Views of teaching vary among cultural groups in the United States, and this may affect the nature of the questions that evaluations can and should ask. The study's first steering committee meeting, with attendance from three of the four sites, was devoted in part to the divergent phase of framing evaluation questions. After introductions, committee members gave brief presentations of how the multicultural initiative was manifested at their site. A discussion followed, starting with questions of impact. The group expressed frustration about how the initiatives were working and suggested that the evaluation should look at how and the extent to which the multicultural initiatives had affected students' lives. Two MSC members took a leading role in the discussion. The first was an African American man fairly new to school one, where the initiative was relatively weak and diffuse. He brought a fresh perspective on school one's multicultural issues. Next, an African American man from school two offered his view as a teacher and coordinator of an Afrocentric education program housed within an otherwise typical middle school.

Soon, a critical underlying issue surfaced. The discussion turned away from content and curriculum to the role of the teacher. There was a sense that some teachers "do multicultural education right," and others don't. There seemed to be a belief that some teachers simply did not understand what multiculturalism meant or, worse, did not care. The committee members present suggested that without this understanding, teachers would not know how to manage their classrooms or communicate effectively with students of different cultural backgrounds. Some believed such teachers, who often sympathize rather than empathize with students, have lower expectations for these students than they would for their own children. These concerns were encapsulated in the committee's question, "How do we get teachers and students from different cultural backgrounds to build a relation where teachers teach and students learn?" A number of other questions related to this issue emerged from the divergent phase of framing evaluation questions.

Between steering committee meetings, the evaluation team began the convergent phase, grouping themes and phrases to arrive at questions the study would actually address. The agenda of the next steering committee meeting included approving this work and prioritizing questions. Committee members from school three, who had not attended the first meeting, were present at this second session. Of all the sites, school three had the longest history of district-funded work with multicultural curriculum and instruction. The evaluation steering committee members from school three, two white teachers and an American Indian paraprofessional/parent, were leaders in this multicultural laboratory school.

As the steering committee discussion progressed, there was general agreement on the language and priority level of each question. A fundamental disagreement arose, however, when the group turned to the question, "How do we get teachers and students from different cultural backgrounds to build a relation where teachers teach and students learn?" To paraphrase the discussion:

SCHOOL THREE: We don't want to impose a top-down model on our students. We want to create an environment where everyone is learning— teachers as well as students.

SCHOOL ONE: Teachers aren't there to learn; they're there to teach. If you tell parents that you're there to learn, parents will say, "Well, what am I paying you for, then?" You've got to accept your role as authority.

SCHOOL THREE: We don't believe teachers already know all there is to know, especially about culture. We think it's important that teachers be open to learning from their students.

SCHOOL ONE: The students shouldn't be in that position. The district provides all kinds of workshops and education for teachers. Yes, teachers learn from experience, but in the classroom, they're in control.

The difference could not be resolved, and the compromise evaluation question became an amalgam of the two perspectives. The phrasing reflected a necessary resolution, but not a refined, easily evaluable question: "How do teachers and students from different cultural backgrounds build relations where the teacher teaches and the student learns in an environment that fosters a multicultural learning community where everyone teaches and learns?" It was clear in the meeting, however, that the teacher-as-authority approach had "won," and the people who had presented the other view gave in. In the language of social psychology, one side forced and the other withdrew (Deutsch, 1973). The collaborative spirit of the steering committee was never the same afterwards.

Dilemma Two: "Let's Get 'Em and Shape 'Em Up." The second dilemma raises questions regarding ethical uses of evaluation and the role of the evaluator or the evaluation team in upholding the propriety of the process while responding to stakeholders' ideas about the information an evaluation should yield. Specific to multicultural education are the social justice ideals that often drive those who take leadership in this area and the professional and personal commitment tied to those ideals.

As we have noted, an issue that became clear to the evaluation team at the first meeting was that some members of the MSC believed specific teachers at their schools were actively involved with competent multicultural instructional practices while others were not. The anger toward those viewed as choosing not to reform their teaching practices—and a personnel evaluation system that failed to address this perceived choice—was manifest in the desire of several committee members for a focus of the evaluation to be "naming" those who opted out of multicultural education and a demand to know why. Our sense was that members of the committee had already named those teachers in their own minds, yet they somehow wanted the evaluation to expose their colleagues with the hope of bringing them into alignment with the initiative's goals.

The evaluation team clearly understood the impropriety of naming individuals, yet its members shared the underlying assumption that a multicultural approach to education is essential to advancing social justice and educational equity ideals. As such, we felt empathy for the level of frustration MSC members expressed. As the planning process continued, the evaluation team and the committee explicated questions the study would answer and adopted multiple methods for data collection. Some committee members remained fixated on the notion of naming and kept returning to this issue. They expressed a desire to include classroom observations as evidence that some teachers were not practicing multiculturally competent education.

Two concerns loomed large among members of the evaluation team. Given limited resources, we were hesitant to conduct observations. We felt there was not enough time to develop and apply rigorous standards for the observations and were uncomfortable with a purposeful sampling method that would explicitly target individuals on the basis of their perceived ability or lack thereof. The team discussed these concerns at the next meeting of the MSC, strongly articulating the problems of this approach. Members of the committee were adamant in elevating the necessity of classroom observations, and the evaluation team reluctantly agreed to conduct pre- and post-observations in tandem with individual interviews of the selected teachers.

Representatives to the MSC each identified four teachers from their respective schools to participate in the classroom observations and interviews—two who they believed were doing it right and two who, in their opinions, were not, for a total of sixteen teachers. The MSC did not explicate criteria for placing a teacher into one category or the other, but members believed they intuitively "knew" who those teachers were and made their selections accordingly. The evaluation team simply received the four teachers' names, not knowing who was who, and carried out observations and interviews at each of the four sites. Our formal research-based observation protocol called for documenting examples of explicit multicultural instructional practices, academic expectations, and social relationships.

As the evaluation team predicted, the results were inconsistent at best. In one case, we later learned, a teacher whom others felt was good did not exemplify high standards of multicultural competency in instructional delivery, while one who was strongly criticized effectively conveyed high behavioral and academic expectations to students and mindfully implemented explicit multicultural practices. Given the limited observation data, we could do little with the results.

Dilemma Three: "Sit Down, You're Rocking the Boat!" As mentioned earlier, the new head of Teaching and Instructional Services funded the evaluation study soon after his appointment. Although he did not actively participate in ongoing management of the study, he was extremely supportive of the work. We routinely sent him information and confirmed that our activities were acceptable to him as the study's sponsor. For his part, when asked he made appearances at two special meetings, where the clout of his position made an important statement of his commitment to those in attendance.

The critical incident that brought this dilemma to life was a meeting of the multicultural coordinator, the TIS administrator, and the lead evaluator. The coordinator explained with excitement that the evaluation information being collected—information that answered questions the MSC had developed collaboratively—would provide specific content that would finally allow multicultural education in the district to move beyond its status as an initiative. (George Carlin once quipped that an initiative is "an idea that's not going anywhere," and in the district many thought the term applied fairly accurately to multicultural education.) The two proposed recommendations for the final report were to (1) create a job-embedded, onsite training model for multicultural education within the district, and (2) integrate multicultural requirements into existing district structures in order to sustain the efforts over time. The coordinator envisioned small-group discussions of the evaluation results, probably by building, across the district. People, she thought, would read the information, discuss it thoughtfully, and then find ways to build multicultural infrastructure and begin to alter their instructional content and practice. On the basis of the evaluation information, meaningful multicultural change could take a giant step forward.

The TIS head almost laughed out loud when he heard this scenario described. "You've got to be kidding," he said. "Do you honestly think this district is ready for discussions like that?" He went on to describe his perception of what was likely to happen. "Teachers and principals in this district can't talk openly—they won't talk openly about multicultural education, regardless of what the data show. Political correctness makes it impossible for people to say what they might really believe, and raising the issue will simply make everyone nervous—or mad. The conversations will be meaningless and are likely to make many people angry." He continued, explaining his suspicion that, given the status of change in this area to date, society might never achieve the inclusiveness that multicultural education envisions.

"Better to be pragmatic about this," he told the two people who had seen the evaluation as a golden opportunity to remake the world. "Prepare a short final report. Fifteen pages at the maximum; ten pages would be better. Then put together a checklist for principals—one sheet they can check off listing ideas they should think about to raise the visibility of multicultural issues in the building. Something really short that won't make anyone mad. Let's face it: everyone likes to support multicultural education in theory, but trying to really get people to change is virtually impossible."

Up until this moment, the evaluator and the multicultural coordinator had high hopes for the project, particularly given the participatory process in which the study was grounded. The incident was critical because it instantly took the wind out of their sails. As it became evident, the TIS administrator, who clearly supported the study—he had funded it and attended meetings to lend his visible support to the cause—had little confidence that the outcomes could make a difference, either for teachers or ultimately for students. His view directly conflicted with the notion that the evaluation process and information it creates might make an immediate and direct difference that could lead to meaningful change.

Implications for Culturally Competent Evaluation

We now modestly present our thinking about culturally competent evaluation derived from this study. The dilemmas document the difficulties our evaluation team faced despite intentional efforts to implement multicultural evaluation thoughtfully. As informed not-knowers, our goal is to learn from this experience and make explicit what we might have done differently. To help the analysis, we turned to two professional documents: the Program Evaluation Standards endorsed by the Joint Committee on Standards for Educational Evaluation (1994), and the American Evaluation Association's Guiding Principles for Evaluators (1995). It is important to remember that the joint committee standards apply to program evalua*tions* while the guiding principles apply to program evalua*tors,* and that application of the latter therefore emphasizes different elements of practice. Table 5.1 outlines the values underlying the dilemmas and presents the results of our reflection.

We believe the analysis of dilemmas one and two points to a pair of lessons: (1) the importance of successfully and explicitly identifying stakeholders' values and interests, the bedrock of cultural competence in evaluation in our opinion; and (2) a conflict between propriety issues (that is, treating participants in an evaluation with respect and avoiding harming them) and feasibility and utility concerns (getting the evaluation done and making it useful). Such conflict is not uncommon, but in a multicultural environment it may take on added significance because evaluators must involve multiple voices, and participants may have heightened sensitivity to their treatment. The analysis of dilemma three highlights a dramatic difference between the guiding principles, which reference the evaluator's role in fostering the public good, and the joint committee standards, which do not. Table 5.1 suggests that in this case the principles for evalua*tors*—to quote three category headings—emphasize integrity and honesty, respect for peo-

Table 5.1. An Analysis of the Dilemmas Using the Joint Committee Standards and Guiding Principles

On the One Hand . . .

Dilemma	Underlying Values One	Joint Committee Standards	Guiding Principles
1	Respect everyone's views and achieve consensus before acting	U4: Values identification P3: Rights of human subjects P7: Conflict of interest	C3: Determine stakeholders' interests about the evaluation D5: Identify and respect differences among participants E1: Consider important perspectives of full range of stakeholders
2	Don't shame or punish individuals	P3: Rights of human subjects P4: Human interactions	D1: Abide by professional ethics concerning people involved in the evaluation D2: Maximize benefits and reduce unnecessary harm to participants in the evaluation D3: Respect stakeholders' dignity and self-worth
3	Work actively to improve the general welfare of this world	—	E5: Evaluators have obligations that encompass the public interest and good

On the Other Hand . . .

Dilemma	Underlying Values Two	Joint Committee Standards	Guiding Principles
1	Get the evaluation done	F1: Practical procedures	B: Provide competent performance to stakeholders
2	Provide information to improve the program	U7: Evaluation impact F1: Practical procedures	—
3	Make reasonable recommendations–small and incremental changes–that are likely to work in context	U7: Evaluation impact F2: Political viability	—

ple, and responsibilities for general and public welfare; the standards for evaluations highlight use, practicality, and feasibility. This points to another lesson: (3) a tension between social action issues and utility and feasibility concerns. To summarize these lessons from our experience, then, multicultural competence in evaluation necessarily involves explicit attention to articulation of stakeholder values, especially when they have the potential to conflict, and to the likely tensions and necessary trade-offs among propriety, utility and feasibility, and social action concerns. Explicit attention to value differences and necessary trade-offs in the steering committee, coupled with purposeful conflict resolution or mediation when differences were evident, might have resulted in a more successful study.

We now believe that certain principles are a given for culturally competent evaluation practice. Everyone should have a voice in an evaluation, but clearly not everyone can have his or her way. The evaluation should not unfairly punish individuals. The evaluation process should encourage and support people to use its findings to create meaningful change. Other ideas are less clear, to our minds, both for practice and theory:

- What if we get all the right groups to the evaluation table but they choose to disagree, refusing in the name of social justice to compromise or even get along?
- What if stakeholders are eager to shame or punish individuals whom they perceive as interfering with progress? Given past wrongs, is this their right?
- How can an inclusive, participatory evaluation process work effectively in a highly structured bureaucracy, especially when the evaluative directive comes from the central administration?
- What are meaningful incentives for people whose jobs are already overwhelming to participate on an evaluation steering committee? To what extent can the larger community participate in a process likely to make a difference?
- What if people in the organization are simply not interested in or willing to move toward a program or society of greater inclusiveness? What, ultimately, is the role of program evaluation in addressing these questions?
- Does evaluation unavoidably support the status quo, or can it be an effective mechanism for leveraging social change?

As is often the case, we ended with more questions than answers. This chapter in no way purports to answer all of the questions about culturally competent evaluation, but rather to engage the discussion and encourage others to join. In our opinion, the future of the field demands nothing less.

References

American Evaluation Association, Task Force on Guiding Principles for Evaluators. "Guiding Principles for Evaluators." In W. R. Shadish, D. L. Newman, M. A. Scheirer, and C. Wye (eds.), *Guiding Principles for Evaluators*. New Directions for Program Evaluation, no. 66. San Francisco: Jossey-Bass, 1995.

Banks, J. A. *Multiethnic Education: Theory and Practice*. (3rd ed.) Needham Heights, Mass.: Allyn and Bacon, 1994.

Bennett, C. L. *Comprehensive Multicultural Education: Theory and Practice*. Needham Heights, Mass.: Allyn and Bacon, 1986.

Cousins, J. B. "Utilization Effects of Participatory Evaluation." In T. Kellaghan, D. Stufflebeam, and L. A. Wingate (eds.), *International Handbook of Educational Evaluation*. Dordrecht, Netherlands: Kluwer Academic, 2003.

Cousins, J. B., and Whitmore, E. "Framing Participatory Evaluation." In E. Whitmore (ed.), *Understanding and Practicing Participatory Education*. New Directions for Evaluation, no. 80. San Francisco: Jossey-Bass, 1998.

Cross, T. L., Barzon, B. J., Dennis, K. W., and Isaacs, M. R. *Towards a Culturally Competent System of Care: A Monograph on Effective Services for Minority Children Who Are Severely Emotionally Disturbed*. Washington, D.C.: CASSP Technical Assistance Center, Georgetown University Child Development Center, 1989.

Dean, R. G. "The Myth of Cross Cultural Competence." *Families in Society*, 2001, 82(6), 623–630.

Deutsch, M. *The Resolution of Conflict: Constructive and Destructive Processes*. New Haven, Conn.: Yale University Press, 1973.

Gay, G. *Expressively Black: The Cultural Basis of Ethnic Identity*. New York: Praeger, 1987.

Grant, C. A., and Sleeter, C. E. "Race, Class and Gender in Educational Research: An Argument for Integrative Analysis." *Review of Educational Research*, 1986, 56, 195–211.

Joint Committee on Standards for Educational Evaluation. *The Program Evaluation Standards*. (2nd ed.) Thousand Oaks, Calif.: Sage, 1994.

King, J. A. "Making Sense of Participatory Evaluation Practice." In E. Whitmore (ed.), *Understanding and Practicing Participatory Education*. New Directions for Evaluation, no. 80. San Francisco: Jossey-Bass, 1998.

King, J. A., Colby, J., Jeter, C., and Nielsen, J. *Evaluation Report on Four Multicultural Programs*. "Midwest City": Metropolitan School District, 1999.

Laird, J. "Theorizing Culture: Narrative Ideas and Practice Principles." In M. McGoldrick (ed.), *Re-visioning Family Therapy*. New York: Guilford Press, 1998.

Lavizzo-Mourey, R., and Mackenzie, E. R. "Cultural Competence: Essential Measurement of Quality for Managed Care Organizations." *Annals of Internal Medicine*, 1996, 124, 919–921. [http://www.acponline.org/journals/annals/15may96/cultcomp.htm].

Patton, M. Q. *Utilization-Focused Evaluation*. (3rd ed.) Thousand Oaks, Calif.: Sage, 1997.

Weaver, L., and Cousins, B. "Unpacking the Participatory Process." Paper presented at the annual meeting of the American Evaluation Association, St. Louis, Nov. 2001.

JEAN A. KING *teaches in the Department of Educational Policy and Administration at the University of Minnesota, where she serves as coordinator of the Evaluation Studies Program.*

JULIE E. NIELSEN *is a doctoral student in the Evaluation Studies program in the Department of Educational Policy and Administration at the University of Minnesota and is a program director at the university's Institute on Race and Poverty.*

JEANETTE COLBY *is a doctoral candidate in the Comparative and International Development Education program in the Department of Educational Policy and Administration at the University of Minnesota.*

This chapter highlights the evaluative process and selected findings from an evaluation of an Upward Bound program. The chapter examines and documents factors and strategies that contributed to the high degree of success experienced in the program.

A Focus on Cultural Variables in Evaluating an Upward Bound Program

Rebecca A. Zulli, Henry T. Frierson

Upward Bound is a federally funded program designed to prepare economically and educationally disadvantaged high school students for postsecondary education. Each year, approximately thirty-three thousand students are served by the more than four hundred Upward Bound programs. Several studies have documented the success of Upward Bound programs in terms of student achievement, high school graduation rates, and college entrance rates (see Fashola and Slavin, 1998).

In a longitudinal study of the Upward Bound program conducted by the Research Triangle Institute that included more than five thousand participants and employed a matched comparison group format, it was found that 71 percent of Upward Bound participants were eligible for college enrollment; the number is 47 percent of individuals for the comparison group. The study also found that 65 percent of Upward Bound participants who were college-eligible enrolled in postsecondary institutions (43 percent for the comparison group; see Burkheimer, Levinson, Koo, and French, 1976; Burkheimer, Riccobono, and Wisenbaker, 1979). In a more recent longitudinal study conducted by Casey and Ferguson (2000) tracking ten years of California State University (CSU) Upward Bound program graduates, it was found that 92 percent of program graduates entered postsecondary education—a rate that

The authors extend their appreciation to Anne Morris, Joyce Clayton, Marilyn Wadell, Artis Stanfield, Shirley Alston, and Ernest Dark for their assistance in collecting the data used in this study. Thanks also to the Upward Bound parents who participated in this study.

is nearly twice the state average. Additionally, at the time of the follow-up, 68 percent of CSU program graduates were persisting toward their educational goals. Compared nationally, only 28 percent of students from similar socio-economic backgrounds earn postsecondary degrees.

Though the success of Upward Bound is well documented, less is known about the factors responsible for this success. All too often investigations into the success of programs such as Upward Bound are limited to examination of services, use of resources, and organizational structure of the program. As a result, the nature and influence of the program climate and the relationship between cultural variables and program effectiveness are overlooked or unrecognized. In the late 1990s, an evaluation of the Upward Bound program at the University in North Carolina at Chapel Hill was initiated. The purpose of the evaluation was not only to examine the program's worth and merit but also to identify the program characteristics to which its success could be ascribed. It soon became apparent that cultural factors were important as well.

In the initial stages of the evaluation, evaluators learned that a concerted effort was made to employ individuals in this Upward Bound program who shared similar backgrounds with the students served by the program. That is, the developers of this Upward Bound program were proactively culturally responsive to the common backgrounds of the program participants. Specifically, they sought to maximize the positive influence the program could have on participants by hiring staff who also shared life experiences with the students. In the evaluation's efforts to develop a deeper understanding of the factors that influence program success, it was crucial to examine the extent to which this aspiration was realized by the program and to examine the influence this practice had on program effectiveness. With this focus on shared life experiences by the program, clearly the evaluation of the program should take into account its cultural context, and thus culturally responsive approaches to evaluation should play a major role.

Culturally Responsive Evaluation

Frierson, Hood, and Hughes (2002) assert that "culturally responsive evaluators honor the cultural context in which an evaluation takes place by bringing needed, shared life experience and understandings to the evaluation tasks at hand" (p. 63). In few cases will program evaluators find such clearly delineated evidence of cultural responsiveness in a program's design. However, quite regularly programs seek to be culturally competent as well as adapt and respond to participants' cultural backgrounds. In fact, the cultural responsiveness of program design often pervades all aspects of program climate and service delivery. As a result, the need to fully investigate the potential influences of culturally responsive program design characteristics on the effectiveness of programs is certainly warranted. Unquestionably, culture is important within most programs, and these authors contend that this fact needs to be fully considered and acknowledged by evaluators.

There is divergence in thinking on whether program evaluations should seek to be culturally neutral or culturally responsive. Frierson, Hood, and Hughes (2002) indicate that the argument has been made that educational evaluations should take into account cultural variables but should shy away from being responsive to them. The example set by this Upward Bound program's developers was not merely taking culture into account but going so far as to proactively build in what could be viewed as cultural responsiveness in program design. Consequently, it seemed logical that the evaluation of this Upward Bound program should not merely take into account culture but instead seek to actively respond to and investigate the potential impacts of cultural responsiveness and cultural competence on the program.

In addition to being culturally responsive in our evaluation strategies, our evaluation plan also needed to address cultural issues as factors of program success. This decision to focus significant attention on culture in our evaluation resulted from our belief that addressing cultural variables attached a degree of value-addedness above and beyond evaluation strategies that merely took into account the dynamics of cultural variables in this program. Merely describing the cultural similarities of participants and acknowledging the existence of the planned match between staff and participant backgrounds without serious efforts to investigate the nature and impacts of this practice on program success would do a great disservice by failing to adequately address the potential importance of cultural responsiveness as a catalyst for program success.

Ultimately, our evaluation work with the Upward Bound program produced important evidence of the fundamental role that a program's cultural responsiveness and staff's cultural competence played in program success. This serves as strong evidence for the necessity of re-sponding to rather than taking into account cultural variables in evaluation. Our evaluation efforts sought to be culturally responsive on two important dimensions: the questions we chose to explore and the methods through which we collected and analyzed data. For the former, we examined in detail staff, parent, participant, and alumni perceptions of the impact of the planned cultural similarity between staff and participants and sought to determine whether cultural competence was a significant factor in program success. For the latter, we elicited multiple data from various stakeholder groups and employed qualitative methods. We used these methods both as a context for interpreting quantitative results and as an aid in developing a rich and detailed understanding of the impacts of cultural variables on program success. To determine the right questions to ask and to appropriately analyze the answers to these questions, we needed to have the cultural knowledge from stakeholders and be able to understand their worldview, and to verify whether our interpretations of findings were valid.

Evaluation Plan

The components of the evaluation plan that made up this study follow, highlighting the purpose, activities, methods, and analysis of the evaluation.

Evaluation Purpose and Activities. This chapter focuses on the aspects of an evaluation that sought to examine the perceived influence on program effectiveness of the cultural and economic similarity of the staff and the program participants. For this Upward Bound Program, concerted efforts were made to employ individuals who shared similar backgrounds with the population of students served. A passage from the program's grant proposal highlights this intent: "To the greatest extent possible, persons employed by Upward Bound will have socio-economic backgrounds comparable to the participants in the program or an otherwise proven understanding and empathy with low-income and potential first generation college students. Student academic productivity, self-confidence, and retention can be adversely affected when staff are not empathetic, lack understanding, and seem uncaring."

Ultimately, however, in practice this stated planned match between economic and educational backgrounds additionally led to hiring individuals who also shared similar ethnic backgrounds with participants. These shared life experiences and similarities in backgrounds were believed to enable the program staff to relate to students and their parents in a way that others from different backgrounds might not have the ability to do. Through hiring individuals from backgrounds similar to those of the program participants, the program hoped to ensure that its staff would have the needed understanding and cultural competence to work successfully with program participants.

To investigate the influence of this shared understanding and potential cultural competence on program effectiveness, an evaluation plan was developed that incorporated exploration of the impact of economic, educational, and cultural similarity of staff and participant backgrounds on program effectiveness. As a means of ensuring cultural responsiveness, an iterative approach was employed to examine the influence that the practice of matching staff and student backgrounds had on program operations and effectiveness. Information was elicited from an array of stakeholder groups, but targeted participants and staff were specifically sought to gather information regarding the influence that staff characteristics had on program operations.

The evaluation did not focus exclusively on examining the match between staff and student backgrounds but instead was designed to examine the overall program culture and climate as well as program operations and services. The plan was designed to be sufficiently sensitive to identify unique contributions of individual staff members and to detect any influences that the planned match in staff and student backgrounds had on program effectiveness. Because the evaluation plan emphasized in-depth exploration of participant and staff perceptions, mostly qualitative methods were used to obtain and analyze the collected data.

Evaluation Methods. Semistructured face-to-face interviews were conducted with all of the permanent program staff—the program director, academic coordinator, program assistant, counselor coordinator, and program counselor. These interviews explored the individuals' perceptions of the program, their specific role in the program, their own life experiences, their perceptions of the program's mission, and their feelings toward students served. These interviews were used in part to assess the extent to which the staff members' backgrounds were similar to those of the program participants. A further aim of these conversations was to detect how the staff members' backgrounds appeared to influence the way they related to program participants. From these conversations with the permanent staff members, personal profiles were created that highlighted unique life experiences of each and his or her personal commitment to the program.

To examine participants' and other key stakeholders' perceptions of program utility and value and to additionally explore issues pertaining to program culture and climate, focus groups were conducted with samples of current participating students, parents, and program alumni. Responses from the focus groups were used to design questionnaires distributed to larger samples of students and parents. The questionnaires, which primarily examined students' and parents' perceptions of the students' level of academic improvement, also included open-ended questions asking respondents to describe benefits of program participation, document beneficial aspects of the program, and make recommendations for program improvement.

Considerable additional data were collected through individual interviews with participants. A series of interviews were undertaken to follow up on important evaluation issues and themes that emerged from the previous evaluation components. In total, sixty-four personal interviews were conducted with participants (sixteen students in grades nine through twelve, forty program completers). To examine stable program characteristics over time and to enable in-depth follow-up on identified issues, the interviews were conducted over three years, with twenty-four interviews conducted in 1997, eighteen during the summer of 1998, and twenty-two during the summer of 1999. A semistructured interview format was used because in addition to gathering information on previously identified topics it permitted flexibility to pursue unexpected courses of questioning.

Over time, the area of motivation became a special focus of evaluative efforts. A key element of the program was to instill in students the "motivation and skills necessary to complete a program of secondary education and to enter and succeed in a program of postsecondary education." As the evaluation progressed, data and preliminary findings pointed to motivation as one area that needed further investigation. The purpose of the interviews with program completers that occurred in 1998 and 1999 was to further investigate the program's influence on student motivation and to identify characteristics of the program's cultural climate that were perceived to foster educational attainment motivation in the participants. The interviews sought to explore in greater detail how the program's services, culture, and climate were designed to influence student motivation, as well as the individual staff members' roles in motivating participants. These conversations explored the completers' beliefs about staff members' perceptions of participants and their needs, and the staff's ability to relate to and motivate participants.

Data Analysis. Analytic induction was used to analyze the narrative data obtained from the various data sources. The data were analyzed by searching for patterns and categories across the responses. After reading through the data, we grouped in categories responses that had similar meanings or that referred to related outcomes. These categorical groups were then analyzed and tentative themes were developed that represented the relationship of the responses in each group. These themes served as working hypotheses for reanalyzing the data. Confirming and disconfirming evidence was gathered, and the themes were revised as needed. Throughout this process the data from the focus group, questionnaires, interviews, and other data sources included in the evaluation were re-viewed to check on the validity of the categories and the themes. Additionally, to ensure that the evaluators correctly understood the cultural context of the program and appropriately interpreted the experiences of the staff and participants, feedback on identified themes was elicited from program stakeholders. This triangulation of data across sources and elicitation of feedback from stakeholders were designed to add cultural competence and maximize the veracity of the findings.

Selected Critical Findings

The section that follows incorporates selected critical findings from the evaluation study.

Staff Profiles. In the overall evaluation, it was observed that approximately 98 percent of the program's participants were African Americans, as were all of the permanent staff members. Moreover, the vast majority of all the part-time individuals employed by the program were also African Americans. Additionally, we found that all permanent staff members not only shared similar cultural backgrounds with participants but were also the first members of their family to obtain a college education and came from similar economic backgrounds as well. Detailed profiles of these individuals were developed to reflect the unique personalities of the staff who drive the operation of the program and to better understand the potential influence of hiring individuals with similar cultural and educational backgrounds that are similar to those of the participants. Here we summarize those profiles that highlight each staff members' perceptions about their role and their similarity to the participants served.

Program Director. The director said that her role was to set "the tone." She used the metaphor of the captain of the ship and saw herself as a motivator and a dreamer who was constantly thinking of new ways to serve the best interests of her students. She took pride in creating an atmosphere of democracy within her staff; she said that "there is no little house and big house. . . . there is equity." She also stressed that she insisted that all staff must be involved with the students: "If it's the bus driver, the bus driver must be a mentor."

The daughter of a sharecropper, the director grew up determined to get the education her parents had not obtained. With the help of a governmental program with a mission similar to that of Upward Bound, she was able to go to college and get her degree. She felt the program's mission was her mission because she came from a background that was similar to many of its participants. She also mentioned that before coming to Upward Bound she was a community organizer. She told us, because she wanted us to know, "that the philosophy of what we are about is a philosophy of living, and I've lived it."

Counselor Coordinator. This staff member saw herself as an assistant director to the program, in addition to her primary role as counselor. The counselor coordinator shared with us that she came from a background similar to that of the students in that she was the first member of her family to get a college education. As she talked with us about the students and her role in the program, she emphasized the importance of caring about the participants and letting them know the staff cared about them. She felt that the caring, family environment was the best part of Upward Bound. She felt that they were constantly challenging students to make the right decisions in their lives. She pointed out, "This is a common message that we're sharing with students explicitly and through our own example we send the message: that you can achieve."

Academic Coordinator. The academic coordinator's responsibilities included ensuring that each high school had a coordinator and supervising the tutorial programs in math, history, science, and English. He was also concerned with finding strong mentors for students. He emphasized the importance of finding people who could be role models and also serve as sources of inspiration for students.

The academic coordinator grew up in North Carolina and was the first member of his family to obtain a college education. He was extremely committed to the program and its mission. This dedication was evidenced by the fact that although he was employed only part-time, he volunteered for an additional twenty hours a week to be available full-time to the program. When asked about his commitment to the program he said, "I've always seen a great need for education. I've seen a lot of young people whose lives could have been enhanced if they had had appropriate education. I've seen children get the most out of their lives. I see a chance for me to help. I grew up without programs like this, and I think there is a great need for them."

Counselor. The program counselor had many responsibilities within Upward Bound and admitted that at times the workload was very heavy and required that he work fourteen-hour days. His responsibilities included supervising the career internships and service learning placements, career counseling, teaching career opportunity classes, recruiting and placing tutors, facilitating selected student summer programs, supervising summer staff, and monitoring student progress.

The program counselor also came from a similar background to the students served by the program; he was the first member of his family to graduate from college. He too was deeply committed to the Upward Bound program and expressed high esteem for the staff. When asked about the key elements of the program, he indicated that the selection processes for students and staff were crucial to program success. He highlighted the importance of identifying individuals who would be good role models and mentors for students and also emphasized that it is crucial that people working with the program be able to empathize with and relate to the students served by the program. Overall, he felt it important that personnel were able to establish a personal connection with students.

Program Assistant. The program assistant described her role with the program as working to ensure that the office ran smoothly and efficiently, and that all office responsibilities were completed. An important benefit of the program she highlighted was that it offered students the opportunity to have someone there to listen, someone who understood what they are going through. She explained that "with ninety students with different types of personalities and confronting different problems, it is important that the program staff be available to provide students with sound, realistic advice that will guide them in future endeavors."

The program assistant grew up in one of the counties served by the program and pointed out that she came from a large family and knows what it is like to have to struggle to obtain an education. She was the first member of her family to get a college education, and she felt that her background made it easy for her to relate to students because she understood what they are going through. She said, "I can relate to the challenges they face, and I can show them the importance of getting a college education because I used to be just like them and look where I am now."

Staff Backgrounds and Their Impact on Service Delivery. Serving as a foundation for all program practices is the staff members' genuine sense of caring and a belief in establishing personal connections with the students. The permanent staff members feel that they share similar backgrounds with the participating students, having come from low-income African American families and being the first from their families to attend and graduate from college. This similarity of backgrounds ensures cultural competence and enables the staff to relate to the students in a way that others may not have the capacity to do. This excerpt from a conversation with one of the permanent staff highlights the connection with students:

I also can relate to the students, because of my background and where I came from, growing up in a large family, being a first-generation student to have completed college. I can relate to them about struggles—what it is like, the importance of getting a college education, staying motivated, persevering, being dedicated and wanting to be somebody, because everybody is some-body, but helping them to know that they are somebody, that you can be a better person, if you are unhappy with where you are right now, just continue to work to strive, enhance your skills whenever possible, when services are offered take advantage of them, and don't sell yourself short, and just letting them know that I care about what happens to them.

In each conversation with the permanent staff about their efforts to motivate students, the subject of caring was spontaneously raised. The staff's provision of caring, support, and encouragement are pervasive program characteristics that the staff attributed to their perceptions of similarity to the participants. Though the program's motivational practices are numer-ous and diverse, they are all grounded in the staff's personal commitment to the program's mission and the participants served. The program staff's personal connection with and commitment to the participants is illustrated in an excerpt from one of the staff interviews: "Our purpose is to promote and be cheerleaders and believers that our students can excel and make a difference and then provide them with opportunities to do that through the activities that we will have and to celebrate them for their uniqueness and for the contributions that they are already making and the contributions they will make."

Participants' Perceptions of Program Influence. The concerted effort to employ individuals from similar backgrounds is accompanied by the belief that these shared experiences make program staff members ideal role models and mentors. In addition to staff members, program documents further indicate that parents and alumni, who also have cultural and eco-nomic backgrounds similar to those of the students, are great resources. Program alumni regularly serve as mentors and motivational speakers and are asked to participate annually in an alumni career fair. An excerpt from an interview with a program completer illustrates that because mentors come from similar cultural and education backgrounds, participants feel the mentors' credibility is enhanced and place greater importance on their advice: "The career fairs always helped me out, because I knew Upward Bound alumni did something actually. They were not just alumni sitting around, and it motivated me because I knew if they could do it, I could do it, and we are all under the same category once upon a time. So, it made me believe that if they could own their own company, I could do the same thing, and they had the same tools that I have today so there should not be a difference between me and them."

In addition to attributing greater credibility to individuals whom they perceive to have come from similar cultural and educational backgrounds, the participants perceived that the program staff had high expectations for them and truly believed that each participant had the potential to be successful. There was also some suggestion that cultural similarity in backgrounds between staff and students led the staff to better understand the participants and helped to counteract negative societal expectations that the participants perceived. This excerpt from a participant interview highlights the suggestion:

> I think that the push that Upward Bound gives us is great. Look around the group, low-income means poor student, so you know [in] our society they don't think much of us. They may think, you know, they a gang-banger or whatever. So if the program sees that we can do better, then why not. I think that push is great. It got me where I am now. I don't think I would be going to State in the fall if it was not there. I would probably be at CCCC working part-time, going to school full-time and driving myself crazy.

Finally, the impact of staffing the program with individuals from similar cultural and educational backgrounds helped to foster the development of a familial program climate. The program director refers to the program participants as her children, and the participants in turn refer to the program as a second family. Some students even refer to specific members of the staff as being an uncle, a grandfather, an older sibling. The family environment also offers the students a sense of belonging and a feeling of unity. The students as a result see themselves as part of a team that works together to succeed. The participants repeatedly indicated that they believed that the Upward Bound staff members understood and cared about all the participants. Specifically, the participants reported that the staff cared about what was going on in their lives, cared about what happened to them, and cared about them as though they were family. This interview excerpt illustrates the familial environment of the program: "They [the Upward Bound staff] can't stay mad at any student. There is too much love there. Like, [the program director] is like our mother figure, even though we don't like to admit it, because she has like long speeches and stuff, but it is just the way she is. She is a mother. She nurtures us like we are her kids."

Additionally, the perceived cultural competence and genuineness of the staff's caring and concern seemed to lead many participants to trust the permanent staff and view all of their efforts in a positive light. For example, when asked about why he thought the program's constant "nagging was a 'positive' thing," one participant replied, "The staff care so much it is ridiculous. They always want to know how you are doing and everything. They just care so much. So you figure anything they are doing has got to be in your best interest."

Discussion

For programs such as those of Upward Bound and others with a strong cultural focus and influence, the findings suggest that program culture and climate may have an enormous impact on program success. In particular, the practice of hiring individuals with backgrounds similar to those of participants influenced program success in several important ways. The permanent staff members demonstrated a high level of commitment to the program and enormous dedication to their jobs. The permanent staff strove to establish personal relationships with participants, expressed a high level of caring toward the students, and worked hard to provide the participants with services designed to best meet their needs.

A second manner in which this employment practice appeared to influence program effectiveness was through hiring individuals who displayed empathy for the students' current circumstances. These individuals felt they were able to relate to the students and understand their needs in a way that others from dissimilar backgrounds were unable to do. This shared experience and understanding also enabled permanent staff members to become strong role models and mentors for participants. The staff members regularly reminded participants that they were once just like them and that they were able to get an education and become successful, and they consistently extended encouragement and support to the students.

Additionally, the similarity of backgrounds enabled the staff to create a family-like environment where the students perceived the staff members as an extended family and where students referred to individual staff members as second mothers, uncles, and grandparents. Findings from the study indicated that the students perceived the permanent staff cared about them as if they were their own children and indeed thought of them in turn as a second family. This finding further suggested that the students also perceived the staff to be similar to them and to understand them. The students believed that the staff truly cared about them and wanted them to succeed, leading to participants being receptive to staff members' instructions and advice.

Finally and importantly, the staff frequently reminded students of their own backgrounds and how they too were first-generation college students and how they had been able to overcome their circumstances and become successful. Consequently, the participating students regularly expressed that the program staff members knew what they were talking about because they had come from backgrounds similar to those of the students.

The students frequently reminded us that the program director was the daughter of a sharecropper, and with the help of a governmental program like Upward Bound she was able to go to college and get her degree. In talking with program participants, it was evident that the participants respected, admired, and looked up to the program director for her commitment to them and for the successful person she has become. It was equally clear to us that they respect and trust her because they know she understands them.

The role of cultural variables, such as similarity of staff and participant backgrounds, in successful attainment of program goals is often not given considerable attention in evaluation activities. Instead, evaluators may attempt to stay culturally neutral and focus evaluation activities on examining program services and service delivery without acknowledging the impact of cultural variables. Because the match between cultural backgrounds of staff and students was a clearly delineated practice that was explicitly undertaken to enhance program effectiveness, this evaluation could not ignore the potential influence of culture on program success. To evaluate programs of this sort and to ignore the cultural influences and the importance of culture is to miss critical elements and thereby render the evaluation study of questionable usefulness.

From our initial interactions with the program, it was obvious that to develop an accurate understanding of the factors that influence program success the evaluation plan had to enable us to explore more than merely program components and services. We needed to investigate the influences staff characteristics (particularly their cultural and economic backgrounds relative to the students) had on program effectiveness and climate. The methods undertaken to evaluate the program proved to have considerable utility since they yielded in-depth information about how cultural variables influenced service delivery and program efficacy.

Ultimately, we found that our efforts to investigate and characterize the impact of culture on program effectiveness were fully warranted. The Upward Bound program is designed to be an educational and motivational intervention program that attempts to maximize the program's benefits by hiring individuals to staff the program who share cultural and educational backgrounds with the participants. It appears that this hiring practice may potentially have a great influence on program success. The findings of our evaluation suggest that this practice has a twofold impact on program outcomes: (1) through staffing the program with individuals who are highly committed to the program's mission, and (2) through ensuring that staff members have the cultural competence necessary to relate to and motivate the participants served.

In analyzing all the evaluation data, a link was evident between the program environment (specifically the cultural and educational similarity of staff and participant backgrounds) and positive program outcomes. Though other programs may provide similar services and have a comparable organization of staff, the unique contributions of the individuals involved with this program and their shared backgrounds with participants emerged as factors contributing to its success. Importantly, it was only through employing an evaluation process that sought to specifically examine and focus on the role of cultural variables in program goal achievement that we were able to document a critical factor in this program's success: the actual importance of paying attention to the culture of the participants and ensuring that the program reflected that culture.

References

Burkheimer, G. J., Levinson, J. R., Koo, J. P., and French, A. M. *Final Report: A Study of the National Upward Bound and Talent Search Programs.* Durham, N.C.: Center for Educational Research and Evaluation, Research Triangle Institute, 1976.

Burkheimer, G. J., Riccobono, J., and Wisenbaker, J. *Final Report: Evaluation Study of the Upward Bound Program—A Second Follow-up.* Durham, N.C.: Center for Educational Research and Evaluation, Research Triangle Institute, 1979.

Casey, C., and Ferguson, D. "The Upward Bound Ten-Year Study of Program Graduates." *Opportunity Outlook.* Washington, D.C.: Council for Opportunity in Education, 2000, 17–22.

Fashola, O. S., and Slavin, R. E. "Effective Dropout Prevention and College Attendance for Students Placed at Risk." *Journal of Education for Students Placed at Risk,* 1998, *3,* 159–185.

Frierson, H. T., Hood, S., and Hughes, G. B. "A Guide to Conducting Culturally Responsive Evaluations." In *The 2002 User-Friendly Handbook for Project Evaluation.* Arlington, Va.: National Science Foundation, 2002.

REBECCA A. ZULLI *is a senior research associate at the North Carolina Education Research Council, where she oversees the development and production of the annual First in America—State Report Card.*

HENRY T. FRIERSON *is a professor at the University of North Carolina in the Division of Educational Psychology, Measurement, and Evaluation in the School of Education. He is also the director of the Research Education Support Program in Chapel Hill, North Carolina.*

7

This chapter shares insights derived from one practitioner's continuing journey toward excellence in mainstreaming culturally responsive evaluation processes, practices, and products. Evaluation's intrinsic value as a self-diagnostic resource for critical and creative reflection, empowered self-improvement, and strategic image management is spotlighted.

Walking Pathways Toward Becoming a Culturally Competent Evaluator: Boundaries, Borderlands, and Border Crossings

Hazel Symonette

In this chapter, I share insights derived from my long and convoluted journey as an evaluation practitioner and as a capacity-building evaluation facilitator committed to demystifying evaluation as a core development resource. I weave in some foundational stories that have shaped and informed my path. Through my work and praxis, I have been striving to walk the convoluted pathways toward being and becoming a culturally competent evaluator and evaluation facilitator. The focus has been on dynamic flows rather than a particular destination status, on a lifelong process rather than a position or product. These dimensions of my journey have often not been conscious, intentional, or deliberately mapped out, but instead more implicit and intuitively guided by a passion and respect for authentic inclusion and responsive engagement.

I highlight examples of one practitioner's efforts to give life to this resolve and put wheels under that vision of provocative possibility. Moving the agenda forward involves cultivating evaluative thinking and reflective practice by spotlighting its intrinsic value, relevance, and utility—most notably, through underscoring the intimate interconnections among excellence in program design, implementation, and ongoing improvement. Rather than an alien, externally imposed activity primarily driven by accountability compliance concerns (*prove*), sustainable engagement in the evaluation process dwells in its *inform* (knowledge creation) and *improve* (ongoing development towards excellence) dimensions. Cultivating the *will*, as well as the *skills,* fuels my crusade: the energizing search for ways to pump up commitment through framing the evaluation process as congruent with the natural rhythms of one's work processes and practices.

In working these processes from the inside out, I strive to ramp up the "pull power" of perceived value and relevance rather than the "push power" of external mandates and fear. My commitment to enhancing the will and the pull power has demanded constant refinement in my capacities to recognize and authentically engage diversity in its many manifestations—diverse persons, groups, perspectives, positions, organizations, and institutions. Through this work, the intimate interconnections between excellence and diversity have come to reside at the center of my life path.

Diversity, in its many dimensions and manifestations, is increasingly acknowledged as a necessary prerequisite for excellence. It remains fundamental for discerning and attaining today's as well as tomorrow's best—our best future. Why? For many reasons, but especially because diversity fires up and fuels creativity, innovation, and generative engagement in all sectors of life and living. For example, higher education, like many other social institutions, is being challenged on many fronts to transform its teaching, learning, and working environments so that they are not only multiculturally diverse in appearance but also authentically inclusive and responsive in their acknowledgment, validation, and full development of the diverse gifts and talents of all. Structural diversity and access issues are critical, but they simply lay the foundation—necessary but not sufficient. Multicultural development requires movement beyond tolerance, accommodation, and pressure to fit in toward a focus on changes in policies, processes, and practices in order to genuinely invite and engage the full spectrum of diverse voices, perspectives, experiences, and peoples.

Assessment and evaluation, when fully embraced, can become powerful resources in this transformation agenda at the micro level of individual multicultural development as well as at the more macro levels of organizational and institutional transformation. Focusing on excellence calls for a vibrantly responsive process that informs and improves as well as proves and thus is not simply an event, project, or product. Again, assessment and evaluation are valuable resources for relevant knowledge creation and for continuous development toward excellence in addition to the more conventional accountability compliance.

Much of the diversity discourse has focused on cultural diversity— broadly construed as socially patterned differences in ways of being, doing, knowing, thinking, engaging. Many such human differences affect critical life experiences, processes, and chances—notably, differential distribution and allocation processes and thus differential opportunities for access and success. Culture is dynamic and ever-changing, so becoming multicultural is a lifelong process. Standing still in one's current repertoire of sociocultural knowledge, skills, and insights automatically starts a downward slide.

Complacency in current understanding breeds and fuels a creeping intercultural incompetence. This "self in dynamic context" learning and development journey is without end in that it summons ongoing personal homework, notably, ever-deepening awareness and knowledge of self-as-instrument and of a lifelong project in process. This complex and often convoluted journey involves:

- *Mapping the social topography.* Proactively survey the shifting sociopolitical and sociocultural terrain—social boundaries, borderlands, and intersections—to surface relevant and salient *differences that make a difference* in access, process, and success.
- *Multilevel dynamic scanning.* Continuously assess and refine your own sociocultural antennae for monitoring, "reading," and engaging in social relations embedded within the ever-present context of power, privilege, and other social structures.
- *Cultivating empathic perspective taking.* Acknowledge and regularly polish the lens and filters that frame your perceptions and meaning-making reflections and interpretations—discover what they illuminate and, even more important, what they obscure or ignore.

The constantly changing sociocultural and sociopolitical landscape ensures that this self-as-instrument work never ends.

When not dismissible in oversimplifying ways as extraneous nuisance variation and noise, socioculturally grounded differences are often defined as problematic targets for amelioration and correction. *Different* tends to be almost automatically interpreted as *deficient* and *deviant*. Not surprisingly, then, patterns of sociocultural diversity have become intimately intertwined with systemic processes of asymmetric power relations and privilege. This has resulted in systematic differences in access, resource opportunities, and life chances. To maximize excellence, then, evaluators need to proactively interrupt the operation of critical autoload or default settings because they result in trust-eroding inaccuracies, truncated understandings, and twisted representations. This is especially likely and problematic when differences are associated with "minority" status, which is almost always treated as deviant or extraneous variation and noise.

Why Bother? Ethical as Well as Quality Imperatives

The American Evaluation Association's *Guiding Principles* spotlight the need to mindfully and proactively attend to diversity issues as a necessary prerequisite for ethical practice. This is particularly critical when diversity is associated with underrepresented minority persons, positions, and views. Guiding principles D and E are especially relevant. Guiding principle D, respect for people—with its focus on respecting "security, dignity and self-worth"—requires empathic competencies in order to offer respect in ways that are perceived and received as respectful. This calls for the ability to engage in cognitive and affective frame shifting and behavioral code switching. Such skills constitute the core infrastructure for intercultural and multicultural competencies. Guiding principle E, responsibilities for general and public welfare, is a logical follow-on for principle D: "Evaluators articulate and take into account the diversity of interests and values that may be related to the general and public welfare." This ethical principle challenges evaluators to *know* the spectrum of interests and perspectives in order to attend to the "full range of stakeholders."

To effectively embrace these principles, evaluators need refined awareness of and openness to diversity as well as an understanding of how to authentically engage such diversity. Presumed similarity through sociocultural invisibility—regardless of intent—is problematic. As the default condition for many, that ethnocentric presumption poorly prepares evaluators to honor these guiding principles in actual practice. What ultimately matters is not personal *intent* but rather interpersonal *impact*. Attending to diversity and multicultural issues in evaluation invites and challenges the evaluation profession to expand its line of sight and the capacities of its practitioners in order to more authentically perceive and receive the voices, vantage points, and experiences of the full spectrum of stakeholders. To what extent do the people that evaluators engage discern and feel that the evaluative processes, protocols, practices, and products are representative of, congruent with, responsive to, and accurately reflect their lived realities—internal sociocultural structures and rhythms (experiential validity)?

Multicultural Validity. Embarking on the necessary sustained learning and reflective-practice journey requires mindful, "light on one's feet" responsiveness to stand inside the internal contours and rhythms of that which one seeks to evaluate. Specifically, it demands proactively discerning and tapping into diverse socially patterned ways of thinking, knowing, being, doing, engaging, and so forth, to maximize what Karen Kirkhart (1995) calls "multicultural validity" as well as experiential validity. Multicultural validity expands and elaborates Messick's well-established test and measurement-related validity domains: "the appropriateness or correctness of inferences, decisions, or descriptions made about individuals, groups, or institutions from test results" (Messick, n.d., p. 1). This and other conventional definitions of validity speak to the extent to which a measurement instrument accurately captures and represents what it purports to measure. Moreover, they underscore that assessments of validity inhere in an instrument's intended purpose, use, and application.

Quoting Messick, Kirkhart (1995) builds upon this statement in conceptualizing the key domains of multicultural validity: "overall evaluative judgment of the adequacy and appropriateness of inferences and actions" (Kirkhart, 1995, p. 3). Substantive content area competencies and evaluator-toolkit competencies are essential in that they prepare practitioners to maximize *methodological validity*—the "soundness and trustworthiness of understandings warranted by our methods of inquiry." Methodological validity includes *measurement validity* (information gathering tools and procedures) and *design logic validity* (evaluation and research design; Kirkhart, 1995).

Though critical and necessary, establishing methodological validity is not sufficient. In fact, competencies related to culture and context are important choice-shaping and choice-making considerations for maximizing methodological validity; however, they are absolutely foundational for Kirkhart's second major validity domain, *interpersonal validity*: "the soundness and trustworthiness of understandings emanating from personal interactions. . . . the skills and sensitivities of the researcher or evaluator, in how one uses oneself as a knower, as an inquirer" (Kirkhart, 1995, p. 4). Each evaluator needs to recognize and polish his or her own sociocultural prisms—multifaceted lenses for viewing, navigating, and negotiating the world within and across diversity divides. Cultivating self-as-instrument and developing intercultural and multicultural competencies is a lifelong process and not a fixed state of being. Because culture is dynamic and ever-changing, yesterday's culturally competent practitioner could become tomorrow's incompetent.

Lastly, *consequential validity* challenges evaluators as well as researchers to mindfully attend to "the soundness of the change exerted on systems by the evaluation and the extent to which those changes are just" (Kirkhart, 1995, p. 4). The modes and substantive content of evaluative inquiry are fateful. The evaluation process itself tends to be a nonneutral intervention. Given these realities, consequential validity calls for socially just changes that are also congruent with AEA guiding principles D and E. Again, the priority focus is on interpersonal and systemic *impact* and not on personal *intent*.

Diversity, culture, and context move from the periphery to center stage once they are connected to hallowed concepts of validity and related threats to data quality and inferential power. They are no longer easily dismissible as discretionary fluff, add-ons, and after-thoughts. They then stand solid as critical framers and informers of professional evaluation discourse, preparation requirements, and normative practices—necessary prerequisites and expectations for excellence in evaluation.

Self as Instrument and Interpersonal Validity. Excellence in cultivating cultural competence demands that we embrace a twofold agenda: inside-out (self-as-instrument and self-in-context work) and outside-in (expanding and enriching one's diversity-relevant knowledge and skills repertoire and one's professional evaluator's toolkit). A critical, yet woefully underdeveloped, segment of needed capacity-building work involves micro-focused assessment and evaluation processes that undergird and support inside-out work. Such work calls for a mindfully conscious self—with expansively refined lens and filters—that enables accurately discerning, navigating, negotiating, and understanding the shifting sociocultural terrain using appropriate codes of engagement. As a border-crossing bridge builder, one develops a repertoire of cues and clues that signal when standing at or in the fault lines of diversity divides. Specifically, what cues and clues telegraph the message "one of us" versus "not one of us"—however *us-ness* is defined? Understanding these in-group, out-group patterns and dynamics is foundational.

Much evaluation is grounded in social relations, and trust is the glue and fuel for cultivating viable and productive social relations. Evaluators need to mindfully attend to trust building as a foundation for quality evaluations because their roles and responsibilities often automatically engender fear and mistrust. Lack of trust erodes the prospects for full access to important data and networks. How and to what extent do one's communications and evaluation processes, practices, and products enhance versus erode trust? Answering this question calls for the triangulation of ongoing multiway dialogues with key stakeholders, especially with those who are being evaluated. (See especially work by Dennis and Michelle Reina, 1999.)

Developing such essential competencies, and being so perceived by relevant others, requires the empathic skills associated with cognitive and affective frame shifting and behavioral code switching. It should be clear that cultural competence is much more a stance than a status, much more about one's orientation toward diversity than facts and figures about diverse places, spaces, and peoples. Moreover, cultural competence is not simply a matter of who one sees oneself as being and what one believes one brings to any given situation—*unilateral self-awareness*.

Even more important for the viability, vitality, productivity, and trust-building capacity of a transaction and relationship cultivation is *multilateral self-awareness*: self in context and self as pivotal instrument. Who do those that one is seeking to communicate with and engage perceive the evaluator as being? Regardless of the truth value of such perceptions, they still rule until authentically engaged in ways that speak into the listening. Bringing a well-endowed evaluator's toolkit is surely necessary but not sufficient. Even if top of the line, it is all for naught if not complemented by *interpersonal validity*-enhancement work, notably, how one uses oneself as a culturally and contextually responsive knower and inquirer. These dynamics are at the heart of border crossings that over time culminate in one becoming a more fully endowed, excellence-grounded evaluator.

Again, most important is the extent to which the meaning-making transactions and interpretations are perceived and received as on-target and appropriate by those on the other side(s) of relevant diversity divides. Those who stand and sit on the privilege- and power-connected sides of diversity divides typically have no clue regarding these dynamics or their implications for social relations and outcomes. As Kaylynn Two Trees puts it, "privilege is a learning disability." Consequently, one may look but still not see, listen but still not hear, touch but still not feel. In contrast, those not so situated within the power-and-privilege hierarchy maintain high consciousness nearly all of the time because such consciousness enhances opportunities for access and success and more fundamentally enables survival. Such divergent realities often manifest in people vigorously talking past each other even when seemingly using the same words.

Investigating and tending to such issues and dynamics is critical among the producers and users of evaluation data, but even more important with and among those who are the subjects (not objects) of evaluation processes and products. To address these issues requires much more than personal self-reflections or even conversations with like-minded colleagues who share similar sociocultural profiles. The deepest and richest insights emerge from authentic communications and deliberations *across* relevant diversity divides. Again, such communications require more than facts-and-figures knowledge and skills or do's-and-taboos checklists—especially when they are associated with making evaluative judgments about merit, worth, value, and congruence. Like any other social relations, it matters who is carrying what and how in determining the extent to which assessment and evaluation processes are embraced as a resource or suspiciously tended to in a perfunctory way.

My Personal Journey and Lifework Agenda

I serve higher education as a planning and assessment facilitator and consultant, along with several other roles. My passion involves mainstreaming evaluation as a process already connected, at least informally, to the natural rhythms of work—notably, making a compelling case to diverse audiences in diverse venues that evaluation is not alien behavior that is solely the province of professional evaluators. I do this through enhancing awareness of critically reflective program development processes—program design, implementation, assessment and evaluation, and improvement—as intimately intertwined, iterative, and developmental. My approach stresses participant-centered assessment and evaluation strategies that inform and connect to all phases of the program, policy, and course development life cycle. Assessment and evaluation have relevance on the front end and the back end, as well as in the middle of the program and other development processes. Ideally, they serve as a self-diagnostic resource for critical and creative reflection, empowered program and course improvement, and strategic image management.

When operating as a planning and evaluation facilitator, I build capacity by cultivating the *will* as well as the *skills* to engage in critically reflective assessment and program development activities through spotlighting its intrinsic benefits. I focus on tools and strategies that help faculty and staff make explicit their "success vision" and intervention activities (program logic models) vis-à-vis progress benchmarks. I encourage faculty and staff to aggressively seize the initiative through using information regarding shortfalls in expected outcomes to map out an improvement agenda. For programs in particular, I work with them to identify their stakeholders and to compile and package compelling evidence—information that makes a cogent case for the success claims that they are making or want to make. This approach moves far beyond an externally driven, often perfunctory accountability compliance mind-set. To demystify this skills-building process and make it less intimidating, I frame the process as iterative and developmental as well as collaborative. From 1991 to 1998, I provided this kind of technical assistance and training for the twenty-seven institutions in the University of Wisconsin System—notably, designing and implementing viable management information, evaluation, and reporting systems. In the next section, I discuss this as a case study—my most life-changing professional experience in terms of my emerging identity as an evaluation practitioner and facilitator.

Since July 1998, I have been serving as a planning, program development, and assessment and evaluation facilitator and consultant for administrative and academic units at the University of Wisconsin-Madison, the system's flagship campus. I also facilitate collaboration across units in advancing the university's diversity strategic plan, Madison Plan 2008, and its general campuswide strategic plan (A Vision for the Future). Being at the flagship campus affords many hands-on opportunities for involvement in program design, development, and implementation in addition to program assessment and evaluation. I have been involved with major new projects from their inception: the Leadership Institute and the SEED (Seeking Educational Equity and Diversity) seminars (both nine-month long, weekly learning communities of faculty, academic staff, and classified staff), the Undergraduate Research Scholars program for freshmen and sophomores, and two precollege programs. In July 2002 I also launched the Excellence Through Diversity Institute, a campuswide, intensive, nine-month train-the-trainers personal transformation learning community and organizational change support network for faculty, classified staff, academic staff, and administrators that also serves as a core leadership development resource for other campus initiatives.

In my broader efforts to breathe life into my vision regarding mutually supportive interconnections among excellence, diversity, and evaluation, I have annually contributed an intensive one-and-a-half-day workshop to the National Conference on Race and Ethnicity in American Higher Education since 1996, the Program Assessment and Evaluation Institute. Within the evaluation profession per se, I have advanced this agenda through serving for three years as cochair of the American Evaluation Association Minority Issues in Evaluation Topical Interest Group (now MultiEthnic Issues), through serving for three years as the cochair of the Management Oversight Committee for the American Evaluation Association's Building Diversity Initiative, and through spearheading related think tanks and capacity-building intensive workshops. In 2003, I started a three-year term on the national Board of Directors of the American Evaluation Association through which I continue to advance this agenda, among others. Through all of these efforts, I seek to facilitate the embrace of evaluation as a vital resource for excellence, equity, and social justice.

Launching My Journey as a Culturally Responsive Evaluator: Toward Facilitating Empowerment

This case describes the spawning of my most intensely challenging, powerfully growth-enhancing and professionally life-changing experiences. It was a contentious crucible framed by the dynamic intersection and interplay of many complex boundary and borderland identities that crafted the sociocultural terrain and context for action—specifically, race, ethnicity, gender, occupational role and status, institutional affiliation, subject matter specialty, geographic location, and type. During my seven years as the policy and planning analyst with the University of Wisconsin System Administration Office of Multicultural Affairs, I promoted and supported the planning, assessment, and evaluation initiatives related to the ten-year strategic plan, Design for Diversity, on our twenty-seven campuses. My student-centered approach focused on cultivating the will as well as the skills to engage in assessment and evaluation, which moved this statutorily mandated reporting process beyond its initial perception as a mechanism for external surveillance and micromanaging control. I stressed collaboration and the primary use of assessment and evaluation as a self-diagnostic resource for monitoring and continuous improvement of precollege, recruitment, and academic support programs among others.

This case spotlights work within the contentious interface of quite diverse organizational cultures, specifically the University of Wisconsin System Administration at the twenty-seven individual UW institutions: two at the doctoral degree level, eleven at the master's degree level, thirteen at the junior college level, and the statewide UW extension system. The individual institutions differ significantly in their missions, visions, program arrays, target groups, and organizational and service delivery protocols and processes. They also differ significantly in their locations within academic and organizational power and privilege hierarchies. It is not surprising, then, that these institutions have various priorities and also differ significantly in their lived day-to-day experiences. Respectfully staying the course in doing this work commanded that I stand (and sit) in the crossfire of structurally conflicting needs and demands. Through the ever-present turbulence at the boundaries and within the borderlands, I facilitated the discovery (or the crafting) of transcendent focal points for consensual joint ventures, or at least mutually respectful processing on parallel tracks. I emerged from those seven challenging years as a more conscious and compassionate border-crossing bridge builder. Though it was initially overwhelming and dreaded, I now embrace this kind of work as part of the natural rhythms of my life and living as a social justice change agent.

Background and Overview

On April 7, 1988, the Board of Regents of the University of Wisconsin System committed its twenty-seven campuses to a ten-year strategic plan for increasing the presence of underrepresented students, faculty, and staff of color and economically disadvantaged students and for creating more multiculturally diverse and responsive educational environments. Assessment and evaluation were integral features of this plan. Each institution developed its own plan in 1989 and annually reviewed and reported on progress in implementing it. In addition to monitoring implementation, they were expected to adjust individual programs, as well as the array of programs that they offered, to more effectively achieve the plan goals. At least once every five years, institutions comprehensively evaluated each program on the basis of previous annual evaluations.

Until 1992, the Uniform Minority Information System (UMIS)—a centralized program information, evaluation, and reporting system—guided campus-level and system-level evaluations of programs for recruiting and retaining students of color and economically disadvantaged students. This system, for a variety of reasons, failed to become the valuable resource envisioned for academic support program implementation, monitoring, and evaluation. The relentless turmoil that I witnessed immediately after my hiring in 1991 led me to conduct a comprehensive needs assessment review of the systemwide program evaluation and reporting process with campus administrators and program staff. That was a wise move because the process revealed many serious problems, issues, and concerns: intense antagonism, suspicions, resentment, and the perception of UMIS as a micromanaging mechanism for external surveillance and control.

UW system-campus relations were severely trust-eroded and contentious. From the very beginning, then, I focused on trust building and capacity building and bridge building—notably, increasing understanding of the UWSA culture, expectations, and needs regarding the wide diversity among the individual campuses. Making the path as I walked it, I expected that this foundational work would ultimately facilitate more productive and trust-filled collaborations and self-sustaining evaluation processes that would support campus empowerment and engagement. I employed a number of key principles to inform my redesign agenda:

• Design a *student-centered* program information, evaluation, and reporting system that "values" the direct student services work of academic support programs. In particular, acknowledge the ongoing tension that academic support staff and administrators experience because of limited resources (staffing, computer support, and so on) in terms of competing demands: developing and delivering services versus complying with external program evaluation mandates.

• Design an evaluation system that facilitates the empowerment of academic support staff and administrators to use program evaluation as a self-diagnostic resource to maximize the short-term and long-term effectiveness of their programs, notably, the educational benefits for their students. Cultivate this perspective: self-study evaluations allow each program an opportunity to speak for itself—offering its vision and interpretation of the facts.

• Design an evaluation system that is responsive to the diversity of educational missions, student populations, and evaluation resources among the twenty-seven University of Wisconsin system campuses. Focus on uniformity of *purpose* in program evaluation without unnecessary uniformity of *procedure*.

Evaluation System Redesign Goals, Process, and Outcomes. On the basis of my comprehensive needs assessment review across multiple UW system institutions, these goals informed and guided my redesign plans and practices:

1. Replace the antagonistic and suspicious mind-set with a collaborative, mind-set and partnership through assessment and evaluation as a "sit down beside" critical friend process—specifically, a sit-in-deliberative-judgment-*with* rather than a stand-in-judgment *of* auditor-oriented process.
2. Eliminate the externally driven, negative incentives associated with the old system (Uniform Minority Information System) and routine, but often meaningless, compliance: notably, the suspicious view of program evaluation solely as an external reporting and surveillance mechanism.
3. Cultivate a vested interest in program data collection and educational outcomes assessment because of *internal* benefits for each campus and program.
4. Maximize the *natural* utility of program data collection, evaluation, and reporting as a campus staff resource for empowered self-improvement and strategic image management: help program staff keep track of the *who, what, when, where, how,* and *how much* aspects of their job duties; and encourage program staff to use program evaluations to communicate their *data-grounded* understandings of how and why desired educational outcomes *do* or *do not* occur for program participants.
5. Establish program evaluation as an iterative self-diagnostic process for continuous improvement.
6. In general, design a student-centered program information, evaluation, and reporting system that is more useful, more user-friendly, more accessible, and less onerous. Make compliance as natural a part of the service delivery process as possible.

By 1995, we had come a long way. My approach fueled dramatic changes in campus and program perceptions and attitudes that moved them beyond mechanical accountability compliance. Facilitating empowerment remained a key principle throughout the restructuring: maximizing opportunities for *choices* among *meaningful alternatives* and providing opportunities to develop the *knowledge and skills* needed for effective performance. At all stages, the assessment and evaluation process and its products were subjected to mutual critical review, campus-to-system and system-to-campus. Campus representatives had a strong voice in shaping our assessment and evaluation agenda— its policies, procedures, and practices. These are some reasons the new system was working even in the context of high-stakes external mandates:

- Developing flexible and responsive assessment and evaluation models. The priority focus was on diversity among programs and institutions in mission, student populations, and resources rather than system-level administrative convenience and uniformity or flagship campus-driven strategies.
- Starting with what campus staff already valued. The *student-centered* program information, evaluation, and reporting system resonated with campus program staff needs and empowered their efforts to maximize educational benefits for students. Framing evaluation initiatives as providing a resource that is "good for students" made it difficult to refuse compliance and still maintain a committed student-focused professional persona.
- Starting where campus staff were and building upon their assets. The critical value of direct student services work and its associated "people skills" was acknowledged while building the case for complementary evaluation skills for self-improvement and strategic image management, for example, hands-on database management training with real campus program data and relevant worklife examples.
- Stressing intrinsic student, program, and campus benefits. The *primary driving forces* for assessment were student-centered and campus-based rather than external-accountability-oriented and compliance-based. Effectively crafting the former—intrinsically relevant program evaluations—laid the foundation for the latter as an important supplemental benefit.
- Using strategies to help demystify and deroutinize the assessment and evaluation process. This involved instituting collaborative knowledge-development and training opportunities, and providing and soliciting ongoing critical feedback on the assessment process and its products.
- Affirming progress. It was vital to be generous in rewards acknowledgment for exemplary campus program development and assessment plans, policies, and practices. This also meant showcasing exemplary initiatives and evaluation reports through distribution to all institutions; showcasing data extracted from annual reports in the *Institutional Profiles* document; and celebrating relative success through "how far we've come" scenarios, given differing baselines and resources (for instance, comparing more recent with earlier annual reports for each institution given the great campus diversity in evaluation-relevant resources).

In this initiative, I focused the UW System Office of Multicultural Affairs model on *outcomes* assessment in the context of *process* assessment and continuous improvement. As a result, we created a much more student-centered program evaluation process, one that was increasingly grounded in conditions supporting effective service delivery. Overall, the process became more useful, more user-friendly, and less burdensome. Program evaluation emerged as a resource for continuous improvement—a critically reflective, interactive, and iterative process.

Conclusion

Assessment and evaluation processes are intimately intertwined with visioning, planning, and development processes, whether explicitly recognized and intentional or not. Excellence demands that one systematically spotlight and then mindfully design, roll out, review, and revise intervention strategies rather than primarily relying upon informal and intuitive insights, or worse yet on default autopilot-type considerations. To do that requires knowledge of what the prize is from multiple vantage points so that one can then keep one's eye on it. In higher education, for example, the ultimate prize is students and what the intervention (program, project, class, activity) envisions them looking like, learning, and being able to do. So, given the relevant sociocultural terrain (context), what are the "program" claims and outcome promises, and how well-grounded and congruent is the "programmatic" transformation bridge that has been developed? Specifically, how viable and on-target, given desired outcomes, is the intervention logic model that connects with the spectrum of relevant baseline resources (assets) and the challenges (barriers and liabilities) that students bring when they start out? In the education sector, for example, this is the key question: To what extent are curricular, cocurricular, pedagogical, and other intervention activities breathing life into and putting wheels under the success vision for *all* students (or other targeted participants)? In answering this question, one needs to be responsive to how and the extent to which evaluative judgments resonate with the meaning making and the lived realities of those who are assessed (experiential validity).

Clearly, evaluative judgments are, by their nature, inextricably bound up with culture and context. So, where there is sociocultural diversity, there very likely is some diversity in the expected and preferred evaluative processes and practices that undergird judgments of merit, worth, value, quality, significance, congruence. Maximizing accuracy, appropriateness, respect, and excellence calls for an openness to the decentering realities and complexities of difference and diversity. Whose ways of being, doing, thinking, knowing, and engaging define the "mainstream" rules, roles, and normative expectations that undergird evaluation processes and practices? To what extent does the involvement of various stakeholder groups call for them to look through *windows,* as opposed to looking in a *mirror,* at processes and practices that are responsive to and reflective of their lived experiences? Like the power-and-privilege realities of other social processes and practices, the burdens of dissonance from window gazing versus mirror gazing is socially patterned and thus differentially distributed.

Consequently, evaluators need enhanced understandings of related systemic processes of asymmetric power relations and privilege, not simply awareness and knowledge of difference and diversity. In particular, how and to what extent is sociocultural diversity associated with patterned differences in access, resource opportunities, and life chances? The presumption of similarity and single-reality theories leads evaluators—as well as other practitioners—to often overlook, if not explicitly dismiss, such diversity as extraneous nuisance variation and noise. Such practices short-circuit the perceived value and validity of evaluation processes, practices, and products and thus erode prospects for their embrace by the full spectrum of stakeholders, most notably those who are evaluated.

My current work embodies an even more conscious resolve to mainstream culturally grounded evaluation processes, in particular evaluative thinking and reflective practice within higher education. In addition to demystifying and providing evaluation training in a variety of venues, I am passionately committed to developing a multitiered menu of diversity-grounded learning and networking opportunities for faculty, classified staff, academic staff, and administrators. Most notably, the Excellence through Diversity Institute (EDI) is an intensive train-the-trainers/facilitators learning community and organizational change support network organized around culturally responsive assessment and evaluation. Cultivating this and other sustained (yearlong) campus workforce learning communities is proving to be the greatest challenge I have faced yet in my journey toward becoming a culturally competent program development and evaluation facilitator/consultant.

Thus much of my current work requires that I stay light on my feet and responsive—making the path as it is walked and crafting the bridge as it is crossed. Nevertheless, with a mindful increase in such developmental practices as part of the ordinary rhythms of professional (as well as personal) life and work, we each will walk with greater and more authentic alignment of our espoused values, beliefs, principles, and commitments. Talking the talk more frequently and planfully coexists with walking the walk. As a result, we will more dynamically self-monitor and thus more consistently *walk the talk* of personal, professional, organizational, and institutional mission and vision. That is my expectation and my hope, and therefore the source of my passion around explicitly and tightly linking the excellence imperative—personal, professional, organizational—with a *mainstreaming evaluation* agenda and a *mainstreaming intercultural/multicultural development* agenda.

References

Kirkhart, K. "Seeking Multicultural Validity: A Postcard from the Road." *Evaluation Practice,* 1995, *16*(1), 1–12.

Messick, S. "Validity." In R. Linn (ed.), *Educational Measurement.* n.d. [http://wwwc-steep.bc.edu/CTESTWEB/whatistest/Validity.html].

Reina, D., and Reina, M. *Trust and Betrayal in the Workplace.* San Francisco: Berrett-Koehler, 1999.

HAZEL SYMONETTE is senior policy and planning analyst at the University of Wisconsin-Madison.

INDEX

Back Issue/Subscription Order Form

Copy or detach and send to:
Jossey-Bass, A Wiley Imprint, 989 Market Street, San Francisco CA 94103-1741

Call or fax toll-free: Phone 888-378-2537 6:30AM – 3PM PST; Fax 888-481-2665

Back Issues: Please send me the following issues at $27 each
(Important: please include series abbreviation and issue number.
For example EV93)

_____

_____

_____

$ _____ Total for single issues

$ _____ SHIPPING CHARGES: SURFACE   Domestic Canadian
                                       First Item $5.00 $6.00
                                       Each Add'l Item $3.00 $1.50
                    For next-day and second-day delivery rates, call the number listed above.

Subscriptions   Please __start __renew my subscription to *New Directions for Evaluation* for the year 2_____at the following rate:

U.S.	__Individual $80	__Institutional $175
Canada	__Individual $80	__Institutional $215
All Others	__Individual $104	__Institutional $249
Online Subscription		__Institutional $193

**For more information about online subscriptions visit
www.interscience.wiley.com**

$ _____ Total single issues and subscriptions (Add appropriate sales tax
for your state for single issue orders. No sales tax for U.S.
subscriptions. Canadian residents, add GST for subscriptions and
single issues.)

__Payment enclosed (U.S. check or money order only)
__VISA __MC __ AmEx # _____ Exp. Date _____

Signature _____ Day Phone _____
__ Bill Me (U.S. institutional orders only. Purchase order required.)

Purchase order # _____
                     Federal Tax ID13559302   **GST 89102 8052**

Name _____

Address _____

_____

Phone _____ E-mail _____

For more information about Jossey-Bass, visit our Web site at www.josseybass.com

NEW DIRECTIONS FOR EVALUATION
IS NOW AVAILABLE ONLINE AT WILEY INTERSCIENCE

What is Wiley InterScience?

Wiley InterScience is the dynamic online content service from John Wiley & Sons delivering the full text of over 300 leading scientific, technical, medical, and professional journals, plus major reference works, the acclaimed Current Protocols laboratory manuals, and even the full text of select Wiley print books online.

What are some special features of Wiley InterScience?

Wiley Interscience Alerts is a service that delivers table of contents via e-mail for any journal available on Wiley InterScience as soon as a new issue is published online.

Early View is Wiley's exclusive service presenting individual articles online as soon as they are ready, even before the release of the compiled print issue. These articles are complete, peer-reviewed, and citable.

CrossRef is the innovative multi-publisher reference linking system enabling readers to move seamlessly from a reference in a journal article to the cited publication, typically located on a different server and published by a different publisher.

How can I access Wiley InterScience?

Visit http://www.interscience.wiley.com.

Guest Users can browse Wiley InterScience for unrestricted access to journal Tables of Contents and Article Abstracts, or use the powerful search engine.

Registered Users are provided with a *Personal Home Page* to store and manage customized alerts, searches, and links to favorite journals and articles. Additionally, Registered Users can view free Online Sample Issues and preview selected material from major reference works.

Licensed Customers are entitled to access full-text journal articles in PDF, with select journals also offering full-text HTML.

How do I become an Authorized User?

Authorized Users are individuals authorized by a paying Customer to have access to the journals in Wiley InterScience. For example, a University that subscribes to Wiley journals is considered to be the Customer.

Faculty, staff and students authorized by the University to have access to those journals in Wiley InterScience are Authorized Users. Users should contact their Library for information on which Wiley journals they have access to in Wiley InterScience.

ASK YOUR INSTITUTION ABOUT WILEY INTERSCIENCE TODAY!